D1331841

THE MERCIER PRESS
DUBLIN and CORK

The Mercier Press Limited
4 Bridge Street, Cork
24 Lower Abbey Street, Dublin 1

© Kevin Boland, 1982

Reprinted February 1983.
ISBN O 85342 683 X

Printed by Litho Press Co., Midleton, Co. Cork.

Contents

Preface

This book was completed in mid-September 1982, before the Parliamentary Party Motion of No-Confidence; before the resulting public identification of twenty-two deputies as dissenting from Mr Haughey's leadership; before the death of Deputy Loughnane; before the illness of Deputy Gibbons: before Deputy O'Leary resigned as leader of the Labour party and joined Fine Gael; before the defeat of the government in the Dáil and before the November 1982 general election. These events are dealt with by means of a Postscript rather than by rewriting where the new situation might require. The readers will see instances where the situation at the time of writing has been changed by these events. I thought it better to let my views in September stand so that they can be related to the developments culminating in the election, which are covered in the Postscript.

As the book finally goes to press there are further spectacular developments in the decline of Fianna Fáil. The new government confirmed a report that the former Minister for Justice, Mr Doherty, initiated the tapping of the phones of two political correspondents and disclosed that the former Tanaiste, Mr MacSharry, bugged a conversation he had with Dr O'Donoghue using garda equipment. These serious matters were by no means the most sinister aspect that transpired. The initiation of tapping by the minister instead of the garda commissioner is a vague technicality, little more than a matter of semantics. Can anyone believe that all other official taps arose from a totally unexpected request from the commissioner, that such a request never followed from a meeting on security matters with the minister? In such circumstances who could say where the initiative really came from? Phone-tapping and bugging are nasty practices but the reason given for this bugged conversation was understandable, if not excusable. The use of garda facilities was silly but it was a minor matter. It was the resulting exchanges between Mr MacSharry and Dr O'Donoghue that disclosed the sinister element. These exchanges established the existence of people, initially inadvertently described as party members this being hastily amended to well wishers who were prepared to provide a fund 'to sort out financial problems within the party' provided there was a new party leader. Dr O'Donoghue described himself as the middleman or honest broker for the well wishers. Whatever about the pro-Haughey members who resorted to phone-tapping and bugging, people should contemplate the implications for the anti-Haughey members of this position; the position that would result from the successful deployment of the funds on offer from this group; the implications for the independence of the party in matters of policy and for the future status of the actual party. The undisputed fact is that these monied people exist and can get a former minister to act as honest broker. Maybe when the campaign to change the leader has succeeded, the national implications of this position in our largest political party will be considered. The process which started with the acceptance of the first big subscriptions has reached its full development.

Almost unanimously the media now tell us that another stage in the trial and error process of finding a leader is imminent. We are led to expect the resignation of Mr Haughey or his defeat on a vote within the Parliamentary Party in the very near future. The successor is to come from the middle ground, a term intended to describe euphemistically, those who might have voted differently last time if they could have done so secretly. There is no saviour there.

1

The Young Men Set Out

'The duty of Republicans to my mind is clear. They must do their part to secure common action along the most likely line of the nation's advance. If you want to know what the direction of that line of advance at this moment is, ask yourselves what line a young man would be likely to take — a young man, let us say, with strong national feelings, honest and courageous, but without set prejudices or any commitments of his past to hamper him — who aimed solely at serving the national cause and bringing it to a successful issue.

'Such a young man examining the situation would see, to begin with, the country partitioned — North separated from South. Here in the Twenty-six Counties he would see an assembly of elected representatives in control of the actual powers of government and claiming to rule by the authority and with the sanction of the majority of the people. Yet he would know that nearly one half of the electorate was shut out from having an effective voice in determining its rulers, and that fully two thirds was opposed in spirit to the existing regime. He would have no difficulty in tracing the anomaly to its source, the oath of allegiance to a foreign power acquiesced in by the majority under the duress of an external threat of war. The pretence at democracy, and the misrepresentation of the real wishes of the people which that pretence covered, he would recognise as the immediate obstacle to a unified national effort at home, the barrier to any enthusiastic support from the friends of Ireland abroad and the screen by which England's controlling hand was effectively concealed from a great many of the Irish people themselves and from the outside world. He would see that by isolating the oath for attack, the whole situation, and England's ultimate control, would be exposed. He could scarcely doubt that, the real feeling of the people being what it is, the oath would fall before a determined assault, and he would set out to attack it as being the most vital and, at the same time, the part most easily destroyed of the entire entrenchments of the foreign enemy. He could see ahead, once the oath was destroyed, promising lines for a further advance, with the nation moving as a whole, cutting the bonds of foreign interference one by one until the full internal sovereignty of the Twenty-six Counties was established beyond question. Finally, with a united sovereign Twenty-six Counties, the position would be reached in which the solution of the problem of successfully bringing in the North could be confidently undertaken.'

The above is the most quoted part of Mr de Valera's speech at the formal inauguration of Fianna Fáil in the La Scala Theatre on 16 May 1926. When the brochure for his speech, which was the centrepiece of the special commemoration concert in the Capitol cinema (formerly the La Scala Theatre) to mark the Silver Jubilee of Fianna Fáil, was being prepared, this passage was selected, under the heading, 'The Promise' to provide the keynote for the occasion. It was a good choice. The young man's appreciation of the position and his planned line of advance was certainly the keynote of the inaugural meeting twenty-five years earlier. That it was also, in 1951, regarded as the keynote of Fianna Fáil policy is indicated by the next item headed, 'Achievement' in the brochure. The following is the record given:

1932   Formation of first Fianna Fáil government. Retention of Land Annuities and stand against British Economic Sanctions. Commencement of Industrial Drive and the beginning of new Agricultural policy.

1933   Removal of Oath of Allegiance.
Abolition of Governor-General's veto on legislation and of right of appeal to British Privy Council.

1935   Irish Nationality and Citizenship Act; Creation of Irish citizenship for international purposes.

1936 Abolition of Office of Governor-General; removal of British King from Free State Constitution.

1937 New Constitution enacted by Plebiscite (July 1). Constitution of Ireland came into operation (December 29).

1938 Agreement for return of Ports, cancellation of war-time facilities, Articles of Treaty and successful termination of Economic War and of Annuities dispute. Election of first President of Ireland.

1939-45 Declaration and maintenance of neutrality.

The first twenty-five years of Fianna Fáil achievement climaxed by the new constitution, the return of the ports and the declaration and maintenance of neutrality, was shown to have brought us to the stage where 'the full internal sovereignty of the Twenty-six Counties was established beyond question'. The obvious implication conveyed by this juxtapositioning of 'The Promise' and 'The Achievement' in the context of the above keynote quotation, was that the position had now been reached 'in which the solution of the problem of successfully bringing in the North could be confidently undertaken'. If confirmation of this implication was necessary — and it wasn't — the 1951 speech, itself, was confirmation.

In the three year interruption of Fianna Fáil government immediately prior to these jubilee celebrations, there had, in fact, been another achievement. This was the formal adherence of Fine Gael — the Treaty party, the Boundary Agreement party — while it was the leading partner in the Coalition Government, to the policy of undoing partition, in other words, to the taking of the final step on the line of national advance outlined in 1926, each preliminary step having been resolutely opposed by them. The following Resolution, having been drafted by Mr Seán MacBride with many trips between the Taoiseach's office and the office of the Leader of the Opposition, was proposed in the Dáil by the Taoiseach, Mr John A. Costello, seconded by Mr de Valera, leader of the opposition, and passed unanimously by the two houses of the Oireachtas.

Dáil Éireann,

SOLEMNLY RE-ASSERTING the indefeasible right of the Irish nation to the unity and integrity of the national territory,

RE-AFFIRMING the sovereign right of the people of Ireland to choose its own form of Government and, through its democratic institutions, to decide all questions of national policy, free from outside interference,

REPUDIATING the claim of the British Parliament to enact legislation affecting Ireland's territorial integrity in violation of those rights, and

PLEDGING the determination of the Irish people to continue the struggle against the unjust and unnatural partition of our country until it is brought to a successful conclusion;

PLACES ON RECORD its indignant protest against the introduction in the British Parliament of legislation purporting to endorse and continue the existing Partition of Ireland, and

CALLS UPON the British Government and people to end the present occupation of our Six North-eastern Counties, and thereby enable the unity of Ireland to be restored and the age-long differences between the two nations brought to an end.

This Resolution was evolved by the collaboration of Mr Costello and Mr MacBride, two of the most distinquished senior counsels in the state on the coalition side and Mr de Valera, the internationally recognised proponent of the Irish cause on the Fianna Fáil side. Mr Costello was one of the most effective and authoritative of Free State voices, Mr MacBride had not found it possible to take part in constitutional politics in Ireland until the penultimate step on de Valera's 'line of advance' had been taken and Mr de Valera represented the authentic Republican aspiration. It was a most carefully drafted document; words were chosen and punctuation marks inserted only after detailed consideration by Costello and MacBride, and de Valera and MacBride. Alterations were made after long discussion and by agreement between the two sides. It was passed without dissent. It is distinguishable from the policy of the present day Republican movement only by the fact that it goes a little further by demanding a British withdrawal rather than

the promulgation of a British decision to withdraw. Earlier
in the La Scala speech, Mr de Valera had said: 'Means must
be found to bring the national forces together — together
at least to this extent, that the two sections will in the main
proceed along parallel lines and in a common direction so
that the resultant of their combined efforts may be the
greatest possible.' Now the means to bring the national
forces together had been found. All political parties had
come together to outline an agreed national policy and to
register it formally as national policy. Not alone had the
position been reached 'in which the solution of the problem
of successfully bringing in the North could be confidently
undertaken' but as the La Scala speech had phrased it, the
people had been 'brought together again for a great
national advance'. All that was necessary in 1951 was effective organisation to ensure that 'the resultant of their combined efforts' would equate with the total potential of the
Irish race at home and abroad, and the latter component
had already been recruited by Mr de Valera's world tour
during the Coalition inter-regnum. The fact that this
achievement did not make the list for the Silver Jubilee
justifies further consideration. Less than twenty years
afterwards, when at last the moment of truth dawned with
the refusal of the coerced section of the Irish people to
accept their fate any longer, the national policy unanimously adopted in less relevant times, was surreptitiously
abandoned under Fianna Fáil auspices and, in 1976, the
Fianna Fáil party was ashamed to publish the history of the
second twenty-five years.

'The Promise' was necessarily abridged in that particular
publication, which was produced as a souvenir programme
of the music, song and rhetoric laid on for the celebration
of the twenty-fifth anniversary of the La Scala inaugural
meeting. It also marked the return of Fianna Fáil to its
rightful status of government of the Twenty-six County
State. The ending of the existence of this state was now the
sole remaining national objective of the party — if one
excludes the restoration of the language as is the normal
practice.

The young man's appreciation as set out in Mr de

Valera's speech of 1926 concluded as follows:

> Were he a young man who believed that only by force
> would freedom ultimately be won, he would be confirmed
> still more in his belief in the accuracy of this analysis. He
> would realise that a successful uprising in arms of a subject
> people is made almost impossible whilst an elected native
> government under contract with the enemy to maintain his
> overlordship stands in the way, with a native army at its
> command. The prospective horrors of a civil war alone are
> a sufficient initial deterrent to prevent any effective organi-
> sation for such an uprising. He would conclude, therefore,
> that the necessary condition for a successful national
> advance in any direction was the removal of a government
> subservient to the foreign master from de facto control here
> in the Twenty-six Counties, and that the removal of the
> oath was the essential preliminary.
>   The conclusions of this young man indicate, I am certain,
> the line the nation will take ultimately. My advice to
> Republicans and to all true Irish men and women, is to take
> it now and save perhaps decades of misery and futility.

This was omitted from the 1951 brochure, as was the
earlier sentence:

> The pretence at democracy, and the misrepresentation of
> the real wishes of the people which that pretence covered,
> he would recognise as the immediate obstacle to a unified
> national effort at home, the barrier to any enthusiastic sup-
> port from the friends of Ireland abroad and the screen by
> which England's controlling hand was effectively concealed
> from a great many of the Irish people themselves and from
> the outside world.

The omitted portions were, in a sense, padding, which in
the context of 'The Promise' in juxtaposition with 'The
Achievement' would, even if there had been room to in-
clude them, tend to obscure the actual projected line of advance and the advanced stage reached by 1951. Nevertheless, it is very important padding in so far as the character
of Fianna Fáil is concerned and it also merits further consideration in conjunction with Mr de Valera's speech to the
first Ard Fheis of his new party.

The remainder of the La Scala speech consisted of a con-
cise restatement of the case Mr de Valera had been making

unsuccessfully in Sinn Féin since his release from prison. Here it met with rapturous, delirious acceptance. It was the picture of the young man setting out on the line of national advance that produced the delirium. The audience was of both sexes, young and old, but they all identified with the young man and, at the conclusion, when the last echoes of the cheering died away, they didn't just leave the La Scala. They marched out, heads held high, humming snatches of Civil War songs, back on course to the Republic clearly charted by President de Valera. They were setting out on the line of national advance and they had subversion of the *status quo* in their hearts. They were people who knew that in measured terms they had been re-dedicated to Pearse, Connolly, Rossa, Davis and Tone. No one had any doubt what had happened. The national movement had re-grouped to complete its task. They would, and they did, tell their grandchildren that they had been present at this great meeting, which was destined to rank with the great events of Irish history and that they had dedicated their children and their children's children to the holy cause. It was the final push for Ireland's freedom. The people would march and this time there would be no one to turn them back with their goal in sight as O'Connell turned back his repealers at Clontarf. After all, their leaders had already weathered the iron hail and no one had heard of Mr Jack Lynch, Mr George Colley or Mr Des O'Malley. The 1970s were a lifetime away as, with their feet firmly planted on the road to being 'A Nation Once Again', they scattered to the four corners of the Twenty-six Counties, the Free State, to light the flame in their own parishes and pave the way for the writing of Emmet's epitaph.

One of the first things Mr de Valera did on his release from jail after the Civil War was to visit the grave of Seán Etchingham but, on this, the glorious occasion of the new awakening, no one thought of Etchingham's warning in the Treaty debate:

Do not have the idea that in one year, or two years, or five years or ten years you are going to have your country free, for if the iron of the truce has entered your souls, after six months of it, and you are not prepared to fight, you will not do so after one year, two years or ten years, when you have Colonial or Free State fat in your bodies.

This, of course, was not applicable in the circumstances of the founding of Fianna Fáil. Fianna Fáil had its charter from the outset, just as Britannia had its charter to rule the waves. Fianna Fáil had its own special group of martyrs to guide it safely in all dangers, temptations and afflictions. Had not Liam Mellowes, whose portrait — for all I know — still hangs on the wall of 13 Upper Mount Street, said, 'The Republic lives, our deaths make that a certainty'. He was right but Rory and Dick and Liam and Joe, the seventy-seven, and many more went to their graves without ever hearing of Fianna Fáil. Still their deaths have the effect Mellowes predicted. So have the deaths of Bobby Sands and his colleagues.

2

Stone by Stone

After La Scala the work of actually constructing the new party began. There had, of course, been a period of provisional organisation, which had produced the delegates to the inaugural meeting. This had begun after de Valera's proposals for a change in Sinn Féin policy were rejected at the instance of the group which had been controlling the organisation while he was in jail. Cumann na nGaedheal had been organised as the new Free State party after the 'Pact' election. A snap general election was called within three months of the ending of the Civil War and about three months after what were to prove the last of the official, as opposed to the unofficial, executions. This was at a time when almost all Republicans with local or national prestige were either in jail or on the run. In these circumstances Sinn Féin had not re-organised and the anti-Treaty candidates were elected under the title 'Republican'. Still despite the difficulties, despite harassment such as the arrest of Mr de Valera and Eamonn Donnelly at an election meeting in Ennis and despite the fact that so many of the candidates were in jail, the Republicans won forty-four seats as against sixty-three for Cumann na nGaedheal in a Dáil of one hundred and fifty-three seats. The Republicans had contested the election on the basis of an undertaking never to sit in the Twenty-six County Dáil imposed by the British with the Treaty and never to take the Oath of Allegiance.

The election was held in August 1923 and it was not until the summer of 1924 that the release of Republican prisoners started. The process was not completed until 17 July 1924. It may be that their sojourn in jail and on hunger-strike enabled the prisoners to take a more detached and rational view than those outside but, in any case, starting with the releases the Sinn Féin policy in the new de facto situation began to be seriously questioned. Mr de Valera took more time than most to make up his mind but, eventually, he came to accept the view that, having lost the Civil War and two elections, and with the Free State administration clearly recognised by the public, there was no prospect of changing the *status quo* through the pretence that the Republic still existed and that it was entitled to claim the allegiance of the people. The argument against the legitimacy of the Free State still remained valid but the view was that this was irrelevant in the circumstances of public acceptance of the imposed position. There was no question of reneging on the pre-election pledge given by candidates but de Valera's contention was basically that Sinn Féin should, in the next election, declare that they were prepared to take their seats if, and only if, the oath was abolished. When his proposal to this effect was defeated, he and most of the others who had been active in promoting this idea left Sinn Féin. Eventually, it had been decided to form the new party and a certain amount of preliminary organisation had been done before the inaugural meeting. It would, however, be stretching things a bit too far to say that all the delegates had already burned their boats in so far as Sinn Féin was concerned before the meeting. Some had but others were there to hear, first-hand, the President of the Republic make the case for the new approach. They listened and were convinced.

The really decisive factor, which swung so many in favour of the decision to form a new party, was the ratification of the Boundary Agreement by the 'elected native government under contract with the enemy to maintain his overlordship'. This was a truly disastrous deterioration in the national position and the fact that it came so early in the new regime made the removal of the 'government subservient to the foreign master' a matter of extreme urgency. With this incredibly docile acceptance of British 'overlordship' no one knew what they might do next. The terrible thing from the point of view of Republican deputies was that rigid adherence to a policy which had not been decided in any formal way could, with some justification, be interpreted as complicity by them in this national disaster. A delegation of dissident Free State deputies had been able to prove to the Republicans that the proposals on the Boundary Agreement would be defeated, if they would take their seats and vote against it. Although a number consisting mainly of released prisoners, were in favour of going into the Dáil to defeat this sell-out — even if they were to withdraw again immediately — the sanctity of the pre-election pledge won the day. The prisoners argued that the pledge had been decided on in circumstances in which it was not possible to consider the position in detail when they were in jail and therefore had not been consulted. It was contended that a unanimous decision to abrogate it in the existing unforeseen circumstances would be accepted by the people, who would absolve them of any breach of good faith. Neither this nor any other argument was of any avail and the Six County title deeds were ratified by the elected native government. The fact that it could be shown that, notwithstanding the Dáil vote, the majority of the elected representatives were opposed to ratification, was of no relevance. The Dáil vote was the official record; the agreement had international status and the position remained so until, by enacting Articles 2 and 3 of the Constitution, the people themselves denounced the action of their delegates. Although Mr de Valera himself was not in favour of breaking the pledge, it was this more than anything else that brought Fianna Fáil into existence. The party arose out of, and was founded on, the shock of the acceptance of partition and on the determination of Republicans to undo it. From the very outset, from the time the party was still in embryonic form, this was the meaning of the sub-title 'the Republican Party'. Everyone in Ireland knew that and there was never any need for recourse to the Oxford dictionary for definition of the term 'Republican' in the Fianna Fáil sense.

After the La Scala meeting full scale organisation had to be undertaken. Rules and a scheme of organisation had to be drafted so that an Ard Fheis could be convened. As the Sinn Féin model was available, it was not difficult to get the organisation on paper. To bring it into existence on the ground was, however, another matter. For this purpose a small organising committee comprising Republican TDs elected in 1923 and others was formed and a few decrepit old crocks of cars were purchased. The committee was under the guidance of the joint honorary secretaries. Seán Lemass was chairman and my father, Gerald Boland, was the principal operator in the field, travelling to almost every part of the Twenty-six Counties and finding that everywhere he went his brother Harry had been before him on work for either the GAA, the IRB, Sinn Féin or the IRA, or for all of the four.

At that time the GAA was much closer to its origins; clubs in all parts of the country were called after subversives and terrorists like Wolfe Tone, Robert Emmet, Charles Kickham, Thomas Davis, Michael Davitt, O'Dovovan Rossa and even the ungodly Parnell while, despite the early take-over by the clergy from the IRB, it is doubtful if there were any clubs named after Daniel O'Connell or Tim Healy — or even after Bishop Moriarty.

In those days organisational work at ground level involved real hardship. Roads were bad and the transport available was worse. Spare wheels were a luxury not normally carried and punctures which were an unavoidable feature on a journey of any distance, had to be repaired on the spot. All the organisers had hair-raising stories to tell of their difficulties in travelling but they generally succeeded in getting to their meetings even if they were a few hours late. During my own experience of travelling to different parts of the country at a much later date on the work of keeping the organisation up to scratch, I often wondered if the practice of meetings scheduled for 8 pm starting at about 10 pm was a tradition which started in the early days. I remember, at an Aontacht Eireann organising meeting in Nenagh, Thomas Meagher and Thomas Gleeson telling me they remembered the first similar meeting for Fianna Fáil in Templemore, when my father arrived on a bicycle which he had brought by train from Dublin and which he used to get from town to town in Tipperary.

The organisers were fortunate in that there was at least one obvious person to approach everywhere they went. Normally this would be the highest ranking, or the best known and respected, Republican officer in the area. The first task was to convince these that their duty was to be part of the new national movement adjusted to the new situation. In most cases this wasn't easy. Many of these 'keymen' were still, in a sense, active in the IRA or on the run. Most of those released from jail went home to try and reconstruct their lives bearing in mind the President's promise that soon the people would be ready again and that their place would be 'as of old with the vanguard.' Some of the best had no option but to emigrate — they knew they were marked men. All of them knew they had been beaten electorally and in arms but all retained their loyalty to the Republic. In most cases, however, the attitude was that, however loyal they might be, there was nothing that could be done now but they would be available when the new effort was made. None of them were politicians. They were men of action, men of violence as historians and outside observers would describe them. Most of those I knew, men like Michael Kilroy and Seamus Robinson, were quiet unassuming people without a violent drop of blood in their veins. It often took a number of visits involving all-night arguments to convince one man. My father had many a long argument with his near neighbour and friend, Oscar Traynor, before the latter finally agreed to join Fianna Fáil sometime late in 1927 or 1928 and it took even more persuasion to convince him it was his duty to stand for election. He had to go at least three times to north Cork before he finally won over Seán Moylan after the latter had returned from America. Indeed, many people were of the opinion that Moylan was never really satisfied in his own mind of the soundness of the Fianna Fáil idea. This is hardly true; he wouldn't have joined and become a candidate unless he was satisfied but he was one of the few who, in spite of full scale involvement in the tangle of politics, was always able to stand back and have a critical look at how the party was developing and where it was going, from the point of view of the founding ideal. My father's great disappointment was Austin Stack. Prior to the actual split with Sinn Féin they had been very close and seemed to be thinking on the same lines. I remember long meetings between them in our house in Marino, when, to my childish ears, the talk seemed to go on and on about going into the Dáil whatever that meant. They had always seen eye to eye, more or less, and had both tried to warn Harry to beware of being too intimate with Michael Collins. My father was still hopeful that Stack would eventually join Fianna Fáil up to the time he died in 1929. Slowly but surely, however, the prominent Republicans around the country were being induced into this new movement and, generally speaking, the acquisition of the right man in an area guaranteed at least the nucleus of an organisation. The next step would be a meeting with a group of the keymen's trusted colleagues and from then on the local organisation would grow. The Republican character of the party was also being consolidated and ensured by the *modus operandi.* The keymen everywhere — even in the cities — were tried and true and only came when they were convinced that the line of advance proposed in the La Scala was, indeed, the new way forward to the Thirty-two County Republic, to which they had dedicated themselves and for which they had striven so hard and sacrificed so much.

Still, it has often struck me in retrospect that there was one very minor but nevertheless disquieting factor, even though it applied only in a small number of cases. My father often mentioned that, sometimes when all other arguments had failed, he would say, 'All right, they have broken their oath to the Republic, they have beaten hell out of us in the Civil War on Lloyd George's and Churchill's instructions, they have killed our comrades and terrorised our families, they have turned the people against us through misrepresentation, they have betrayed the national cause and, in particular, the Six Counties, all for a British bribe. Are you going to sit back and let them enjoy the fruits of their treachery?' There were, of course, a number of Cumann na nGaedheal leaders who were prominent in the struggle all the way through but, more often than not, when a man looked around him, he would see that the people enjoying the fruits of office were mere 'trucers' as those who joined during the Truce were called, or even worse, Redmondites. And, sometimes when everything else had failed, the answer to this last harrangue would be, 'No, by God I am not'. There was no unworthy motive involved at the time but, in practice, the only way to deprive the wrong-doer of the fruits of his misdeeds is, often, to acquire them for oneself. It is, of course, perfectly clear that the disappearance of idealism from Fianna Fáil came with the new recruits whose advent was at a much later stage and was to the party of power, the party of reality, the party of pragmatism rather than to the Republican party but, at the same time, one wonders, if the seeds of deterioration were not already there from the co-existence, with the idealism, of the less than noble motive of depriving the turncoats of the fruits of office, which was the clinching argument in a small minority of cases.

Whatever about this more materialistic motive in the background, all the membership joined as Republicans to turn defeat into ultimate victory and, above all, to restore the unity of the country. In a short time they constructed an organisation that has never been equalled in this country. They went through difficult times when adherence to the Republican ideal was sorely tested and other times when they found it difficult to reconcile adherence to this ideal with adherence to Fianna Fáil. They were highly disciplined and understood that personal interests often had to be subordinated to the national interest and the national interest was the 'line of advance' put forward at the La Scala meeting. Everything was subordinated to that and this was the motivation that maintained their morale through thick and thin. They voted and canvassed exactly as the strategists at national and local level planned. In the early days candidates were not allowed to canvass at all. In many rural constituencies in particular, the constituencies were divided among the candidates with mathematical accuracy and there were no breaches of the plan. The candidates themselves having almost all been comrades in arms worked as a team. The outstanding example of this was in Kerry, which, probably because of the memory of the Free State reign of terror in the county, remained a predominantly Republican county up to quite recent times. Here, after Sinn Féin, and therefore Austin Stack, stopped contesting elections, Fr Allman divided the original seven seat constituency with great accuracy and skill between his team of candidates. The organisation and the panel of candidates were so disciplined that the supporters voted almost exactly as advised and the whole panel were always in a solid block with a small difference between the highest and the lowest. The results progressed from the last four seats (with the fifth behind by a nose) in the second 1927 election, when Sinn Féin support was not all mobilised in time, to the first five seats in 1932 and 1933. This continued into the new north Kerry and south Kerry constituencies until 1943 when other considerations affecting overall support intervened and when it was already twenty years from the Martyrdom of Kerry.

Once a reliable and influential local Republican was recruited he would be given the task of building the organisation on the ground in his area and the headquarter's committee would send representatives to meetings and generally supervise the development of the organisation in each constituency until it was fully covered. After the first organisation drive there was never a period when the organisation was deficient and later re-organisation campaigns were mainly concerned with adjustments required for constituency changes and with rationalisation in view of rural depopulation, which, strangely for an increasingly pragmatic party, was most marked in the western Republican areas. The first Ard Fheis was held on 24 November 1926 with all parts of the Twenty-six Counties well represented. The picture was of a party effectively organised in a remarkably short space of time but, of course, still with a lot of consolidation to be done. The Ard Fheis was unambiguously Republican in the special Irish sense of the word. The only real difference with Sinn Féin was in the matter of tactics. There was no acceptance of the legitimacy of the Free State, which had been officially characterised at the La Scala as a 'pretence at democracy'. It was merely a question of recognising the *de facto* situation for practical reasons. It is certain that not all delegates had severed their connection with the IRA, who were once again expected to be in the vanguard, and, indeed, it is probable that some had not formally broken with Sinn Féin. Nevertheless, while there were some, who were still keeping their options open, they were all enthusiastic about the new venture and it was a remarkable achievement to have produced, in a matter of months, such a comprehensive organisation out of the deep post-Civil War disillusionment. The slowness of some in breaking with Sinn Féin arose partly from sentiment and partly from the need to be absolutely sure about the new party.

3

Built-in Ambivalence

Fianna Fáil are often accused of being ambivalent about the use of force. For many years past this has always been hotly, and incorrectly, denied and an attempt has been made to establish as fact the demonstrably false pretence that the party's opposition to the use of force has always been total and uncompromising. This is nonsense. Furthermore it is based on the contention, which is now fashionable, that nothing is ever achieved by violence. All human history establishes this as arrant nonsense and, indeed, the existence of the Six Counties as a separate entity is, in itself, testimony to the efficacy of threatened violence as opposed to democracy. The only honest reply to the charge of a certain element of ambivalence in regard to the use of force is to admit that this was built in to the new Republican party from the beginning. When Neil Blaney said in Letterkenny on 8 December 1969 that de Valera had never categorically ruled out force in all circumstances, he was stating an easily verifiable fact. What was always ruled out was the use of force to establish unity and this policy was, in fact, a continuation of the policy in this regard adopted by Sinn Féin in 1921. The establishment of unity was recognised as a problem, which could only be exacerbated by the use of force to solve it but it was always made clear that the international problem of the continued holding of part of Ireland by Britain was a different matter. This was a continuing injustice and aggression by Britain against the Irish nation, which had to be ended before any progress towards unity could be made. In the *de facto* circumstances, which had been established by force, the threat of force and by deception, the use of force, even for this purpose, either by the Twenty-six Counties or the coerced people in the Six Counties, was considered inadvisable but there was never any question of denying that the Six County nationalists had the same right as the Irish people as a whole always had to break the connection with England. At no time did the circumstances change so as, in Fianna Fáil's estimation, to justify resort to force but it was unthinkable that the Twenty-six County security forces would ever be used to enforce British rule in the Six Counties except by a 'government under contract with the enemy to maintain his overlordship'. This attitude remained right through the period of confrontation with the militant Republican movement until Mr Lynch got rid of the Republican remnant of his government in 1970. Then the whole parliamentary party without exception accepted the role of joint-enforcers with Her Majesty's government of what used to be 'the gravest injury one nation could inflict upon another' and the whole organisation, which had been built in every part of the Twenty-six County State for the express purpose of ending this injustice, also accepted this role with only minimal refusals. Most of the few, who could not bring themselves to turn on their own people in the Six Counties, as loyalty to Fianna Fáil now required, just retired from active membership and left the field to the new collaborators. This change could not and did not come overnight. Obviously, the Republican principle had been gradually eroded over a period and had become merely an outmoded catchcry, which rallied a certain unknown percentage of the electorate to the colours in all circumstances. Free State fat had been accumulating. Fianna Fáil had not adopted the Fine Gael policy: they had adopted the old Cumann na nGaedheal policy. In fairness to the grass roots membership, it must be remembered that Mr de Valera senior had left a son in the Dáil (and in the *Irish Press*) to provide continuity of principle. There was never one solitary whimper of protest, criticism or doubt from that source and de Valera himself, who in other less relevant times had left the Republican case on record all round the world, continued on as President of the Twenty-six County State and as commander-in-chief of the army which was acting in full support of the British effort to impose a military solution. He remained, giving every indication of support for the new policy of Fianna Fáil until he ceased to be President with the effluxion of time — and then he retired with his long life's work done, with his earlier words firmly on record uncontradicted except by his latter-day actions or inaction and with no comment on the travail of the abandoned section of the national majority on their native heath in the Six Counties. Even then, apparently, he had not come to the conclusion that the gospel he had preached all his life was so wrong that it called for public retraction. The people, in Ireland and America who had been so consistently harangued for two generations, were, in the hour of crisis, left to form their own opinions and make their own decisions without guidance.

In the first chapter of this book I have quoted the young man's appreciation of the situation in 1926 in full and suggested that the parts omitted in the 1951 document, to which I referred, should be considered in conjunction with Mr de Valera's speech at the first Ard Fheis five months later. The relevant passage in this speech is:

> It is vain to think that the natural aspirations of Irishmen for the liberty of their country are going to be stifled now. If the road of peaceful progress and natural evolution be barred, then the road of revolution will beckon and will be taken. Positive law and natural right will be involved in the old conflict. The question of majority rule and minority right will be again bloodily fought out, and when the fight is over it will probably be found out once more that the problem has remained and that force is not the solution. It is in the hope that we shall be able to rescue our people from that fate that we are met here today to band ourselves together.
>
> I have never said, and am not going to say now, that force is not a legitimate weapon for a nation to use in striving to win its freedom. I know that in history it is seldom that foreign tyrants have ever yielded to any other. I have believed and still believe, that if a nation held in subjection by a foreign power were to exclude altogether the idea of using physical force to free itself, it would in effect be handing itself over as a bound slave without hope of redemption. It is a long wait they destine themselves to who rely on their tyrants suffering a change of heart.

In the La Scala speech the Free State parliament is described as 'the pretence at democracy' and the government's control is unambiguously characterised as *de facto* control. The proposal to enter the Dáil at the outset was to take part, as people whose allegiance was to the democratically established Republic, in an assembly of the elected representatives of the Twenty-six Counties. Seán Lemass, later regarded as the supreme pragmatist described Fianna Fáil as a 'slightly constitutional party' and, indeed, although Fianna Fáil having secured 'the removal of the government subservient to the foreign master from *de facto* control here in the Twenty-six Counties', exercised the powers of government from 1932, the original attitude to the Dáil was never publicly renounced until the enactment of the new constitution which created a new situation and a new Dáil. From then on there could be no doubt, in the mind of any reasonable person, of the legitimacy of the elected government. For instance, it was only then that Mr Seán MacBride decided that to take part in constitutional politics was consistent with loyalty to the Republic. The people enacted the Constitution and it was from the people only power derived. The national territory was accurately defined and the status of the Six Counties was that it was part of the national territory in which jurisdiction was not exercised pending re-unification. There was no longer any ambivalence about the IRA — they were an anachronism in the new situation, but it was clearly stated in the Constitution itself that the laws of the State applied only in the Twenty-six Counties 'pending the re-integration of the national territory'. How, then, one may ask, can a person be held to be in breach of Irish law by the offence of being a member in the Six Counties of an organisation which is illegal in this State? In these circumstances the government could advise the coerced people in the Six Counties, but the Constitution surely rules out any attempt to compel them to act in accordance with that advice. The national territory has not been integrated. The Six Counties is outside the jurisdiction and so is the mainland of Britian. To me, as a layman, it appears that the Constitution specifies the area in which the laws enacted by the Irish parliament apply and also that the courts are authorised to enforce these laws only. It beats me how they can be held to have the authority to enforce the laws of another country in respect of activities alleged to have taken place in the territory of that country, without being given that authority by the Constitution. The function of the courts is described as the 'administration of justice' but, surely, justice in this context is defined by the laws of the State, not by the laws of another State? If it is held that, legalistically, the Constitution does not rule out the enforcement of the laws of Her Majesty's government, by the Irish courts on Irish citizens in respect of offences committed on the 'mainland' or in the part of the National Territory of Ireland which is still pending reintegration, this is obviously because such an eventuality stood not within the prospects of belief. This, of course, has not been tested and we don't know whether it is legal or not.

Mr de Valera said at the first Ard Fheis:

> I have believed and still believe, that if a nation held in subjection by a foreign power were to exclude altogether the idea of using physical force to free itself, it would in effect be handing itself over as a bound slave without hope of redemption. It is a long wait they destine themselves to who rely on their tyrants suffering a change of heart.

In the Six Counties the long wait, to which the acceptance of the Free State had destined them, had been experienced; there was no change in the position; and the statement was never retracted. It always remained the Fianna Fáil position until the party and its members submitted themselves to the sole personal control of a man who had to have recourse to a dictionary to define the term 'Republican' because, up to then, he had never had occasion to enquire what Fianna Fáil was all about. The Irish nation consciously destined itself to a long wait but did not hand itself over as 'a bound slave without hope of redemption'. We have experienced sixty-two or sixty or fifty-seven years of British intransigence, depending on whether we start in 1920, 1922 or 1925, and the British capacity for resisting moral persuasion, for ignoring the principles of justice and democracy, seems to be infinite in the absence of the catalyst of force or threatened force, which has proved necessary in every part of the erstwhile empire. Sir Harold

Wilson, Edward Heath, Jim Callaghan and Margaret Thatcher have all shown the same determination to resist the according of justice to Ireland as Sir Robert Peel demonstrated so effectively to O'Connell's peaceful monster meetings. The Argentine has had the same experience in the case of Las Malvinas. Who can blame her for introducing the catalyst, in a low key manner, when it was obvious that the British intention was to procrastinate indefinitely as long as only peaceful methods were relied on? And when the Fianna Fáil party in 1970 withdrew the national claim proclaimed all over the world by de Valera and formally adopted unanimously by Dáil Éireann, can history blame the section of the nationalist majority who, being temporarily outside the jurisdiction, acted in accordance with de Valera's solemnly declared belief in 1926? The road of peaceful progress and national evolution was barred mainly by Fianna Fáil's defection, and the road of revolution beckoned as de Valera said it would, and it was taken — as de Valera said it would. The taking of this road may have been contrary to the wishes of the Irish government but the road did not cross the Border and it was not in breach of the Irish laws, which extended only to the area of Saorstat Éireann.

Ambivalence may not be the perfect word to describe the attitude to force outlined and unanimously adopted by acclamation at the inaugural meeting and at the first Ard Fheis but it is a reasonable description of it. Mr de Valera at no point put forward the idea of force as a policy for Fianna Fáil but, unlike O'Connell, he always made it clear that it could never be excluded, if there were to be any hope of success. At the very outset he stated in the clearest terms that one of the reasons making 'the removal of a government subservient to the foreign master from *de facto* control' essential was that the existence of such an elected native government made a successful uprising almost impossible. Surely it follows from this that, when this elected government was removed, one of the national benefits gained was that now a successful uprising was no longer almost impossible? Fianna Fáil was constituted with this ambivalence and most political observers would say that it has not completely disappeared yet despite twelve years of full-scale participation in the British war effort, twelve years of total alliance, making us jointly responsible for police and military brutality, official terrorisation of the nationalist community, torture, Bloody Sunday, the hunger-strike deaths, plastic bullets and the immunity granted to the British soldiery for blatant murder of innocent civilians. There was nothing incongruous or inconsistent in this Fianna Fáil ambivalence in view of the successful, vicious, British stratagem of inserting two elected Irish governments between themselves and the aspiration of the Irish Nation — a stratagem designed to make indefinite resistance to Ireland's claim for justice and democracy, feasible. The artificial maintenance of a tiny colonial community as the sole inhabitants of Las Malvinas was a similar typically unscrupulous and ingenious imperialist stratagem to facilitate interminable resistance to the justice and logic of the Argentinian claim, which is really for the rationalisation of this part of the South Atlantic now that the British Empire is a thing of the past. It is an area in which there is no conceivable justification for a British presence and British withdrawal is essential to international stability.

The young man, on whose appreciation of the Irish situation the Fianna Fáil line of national advance was based, was quite clearly visualised as being very possibly if not probably a young man who believed that only by force would freedom ultimately be won. The party did not really distance itself from the IRA until the actual break came with the IRA decision to embark on hostile action against Britain, a decision which was notified to the government and to which the government could not and did not attempt to close its eyes. Immediately prior to this, the IRA had been helpful in defeating the Blueshirt violence and this help had not been spurned. If Fianna Fáil were ambivalent to the IRA, the latter were also ambivalent to them. Many of the Civil War veterans, who remained active in the IRA, had for a number of years almost as much contact with Fianna Fáil politicians as with Sinn Féin politicians. The 'Broy harriers' were, in fact, recruited almost directly from the IRA to make up for the possible lack of enthusiasm and dragging of feet by sections of the Garda Síochana inherited from the Cumann na nGaedheal government in dealing with the Blueshirt campaign to bring down the government by undemocratic means. Almost all Ministers recruited their official drivers from their own IRA units and, in any case where this was not done, the deficiency was supplied by men who had served with the then Minister for Defence, Mr Aiken.

I need go no further in considering this attitude popularly classified as ambivalence than my own father. He was the prototype of the Irishman born and bred in the physical force tradition and in the authentic Republican tradition of the United Irishmen. He had the contempt of John Mitchel for O'Connell and a most comprehensive knowledge of and contempt for the anti-national record of the Irish hierarchy. He accepted excommunication as a matter of course and virtually as an authentication of the correctness of his political approach. It was part of his Republican heritage. He joined the IRB at the earliest age at which he would be accepted and left it after 1916. In the 1940s, as Minister for Justice, he was the instrument of the Fianna Fáil suppression of the IRA, a role he undertook only when he himself was fully convinced that this was not only justified but that it was his personal national duty and he carried out this role without ambivalence. Yet, sometime before he died, he told me that even throughout this period he always admired them although he thoroughly disagreed with them and, in 1970, he publicly stated that, in the then existing circumstances the government should be training commando type groups to operate in support of the besieged nationalist community in the Six Counties. This is exactly what any sovereign government in the world with a legitimate territorial claim would have been doing, in case the situation developed as appeared to be almost certain. In fact, as emerged clearly in court in 1970, the Fianna Fáil government did move some distance towards this by starting to provide some training for Six County people in the techniques of defensive street fighting. This was well before the Taoiseach's sudden volte face in the matter of the attempted arms importation. It was not connected with this particular incident and was mentioned without any de-murral at a government meeting. By all the long-estab-lished standards of Fianna Fáil it was, at that time, their historic duty to prepare for the possibility that such assistance might be required and, again, it was established in court that there was a formal delegation of authority to the Ministers for Defence and Finance to make such preparations and that this decision was conveyed to the army chief-of-staff. Obviously, then, the established Fianna Fáil attitude was presumed by the government still to exist until the Taoiseach gradually disclosed that, as far as he was concerned, partition was for keeps. Why argue about the appropriateness of the term 'ambivalence'? The fact is that the Fianna Fáil attitude to force was an integral part of the party; it was always understood to be as de Valera prescribed it at the outset and it was perfectly logical. If illogicality is an inherent quality of ambivalence then the term is not accurate in this context. Violence would never have played a significant part in the final solution of the Irish-British problem, which is now being processed so violently, were it not for the retraction by Fianna Fáil of all the principles it had enunciated to all the Irish race, at home and abroad, for almost half a century.

To the best of my knowledge the first aim of Fianna Fáil still is 'to secure the unity and independence of Ireland as a Republic'. This gives the definition of the term 'Republican' as it is used in the sub-title — The Republican Party. I feel sure this definition does not appear in any dictionary so it may not be quite fair to blame Mr Lynch for not knowing it. Still, one would imagine that, even in the run-up to the fiftieth anniversary, there would still be someone around to tell him. The first election manifesto published by Fianna Fáil devotes an entire page to the following:

The following is the Pledge which must be taken by each Candidate put forward for Parliamentary Elections by Fianna Fáil:

I .... hereby undertake that if elected to the office of .... I will support Fianna Fáil (Republican Party) in every action it takes to secure the

Independence of a United Ireland under a Republican form of Government, and, in accordance with its constitution, I will not take any position involving an oath of allegiance to a foreign power and I further undertake that if called upon by a two-thirds majority of the National Executive of Fianna Fáil to resign that office, I shall immediately do so.

Elected candidates were required to undertake to support the party only in 'every action it takes to secure the Independence of a United Ireland under a Republican form of Government'. This is incontrovertible evidence of the primacy of the first aim and of the fact that it was the essential element in the character of the party. It was the reason for the existence of the party, its motivating force. It was the cementing force which kept people of different backgrounds and different social and economic outlooks united. Above all it was the ingredient, which made the organisation virtually unbeatable, its morale unshakable and its resilience inexhaustible. It was not a normal political party because it had this noble and historic ideal. It was the national movement. No member had any doubt about that. They had set out from the La Scala on the line of national advance and the winning of elections was essential to that advance. That was why they won them and why the occasional defeat — regarded as a temporary aberration by the people — had a revivifying effect. They were on the march, still with the same enthusiasm and the same grim determination as in 1926. The subsequent extension of the pledge to cover all actions of the party arose from experience of the exigencies of practical politics, that is to say, from the accumulation of Free State fat but, in so far as the organisation was concerned, the first aim was supreme. It had been so ordained at the beginning and it stood them in good stead for many a year and in many a difficulty.

Fianna Fáil Republicanism always recognised that unity required a change of attitude by the unionists and that not alone was force incapable of producing such a change but, even if it were feasible, it would be undesirable and unjustifiable. It is often said that no effort was made to bring about such a change. This is not quite true but it is certain that the main thrust was against the injustice and breach of democracy inherent in the imposed solution. This was seen as the first target, the first hurdle to be crossed and it would be folly to confuse the issue. To do this would play into the hands of the British strategists who planned to keep the problem permanently unsolved by using the complicating factor of the disaffected minority — in other words by playing the Orange card. Mr de Valera did not fall into this trap but kept to the ending of the 'gravest injustice one nation could inflict on another' as the first essential. It was always seen that no progress could be made in the solution of the internal Irish problem until the international problem had been disposed of. As long as the British connection was there, the Irish problem was in perpetual stalemate. Surely the last fourteen years have demonstrated the truth of this? There are two stages and the second stage cannot begin until the first is accomplished. British legislation, the British crown, British subsidisation and above all the British army stand between the two estranged sections of the Irish nation and keep them immovably apart. Each step taken by successive Irish governments in developing collaboration to the present united British-Irish effort, has been seen as a sign of weakness by our nearest and dearest EEC partner — the foreign enemy of 1926, who has made no solitary move of conciliation since then. There has been no British movement, not an inch and, naturally, each step taken by the Irish government has consolidated unionist determination to hang on to the status quo. Todays's words from the adamantine lips of Mrs Thatcher are the same as Sir Robert Peel's response to Daniel O'Connell. Mr de Valera, and therefore Fianna Fáil, always realised that there would almost certainly have to be an interim arrangement between the achievement of the first stage and the achievement of the second stage. Whether the party as a whole really appreciated the nature of the concessions that would be required is doubtful. Some certainly did but it is probably true that the majority did not really appreciate what would be necessary to accommodate Tone and Davis as first class citizens — not to mention the Orange Order,

which is an integral part of the Irish nation and whose trad-
ditions and culture are part of the complex traditions and
culture of Ireland.

4

The Seven Aims

The original Fianna Fáil party had other distinguishing characteristics. It was unmistakably a small man's party, radical, left of centre, but it would never have qualified as socialist. It did not, of course, ever purport to be socialist but until comparatively recent years it always maintained that, Fianna Fáil policy being as it was, there was no need for a Labour party. Generally speaking, this was widely accepted by the public and it is only now that the people are beginning to appreciate the change that has taken place in this regard. Their trade union officials are not active in Fianna Fáil as many of them used to be, but their bosses are. It is hard to believe it now but in its initial phase in opposition and in government right up to the Second World War the party showed every sign of genuinely relating its policy to the seven aims enshrined in the Coru. These were and probably still are:

1. To secure the Unity and Independence of Ireland as a Republic
2. To restore the Irish language as the spoken language of the people and to develop a distinctive national life in accordance with Irish traditions and ideals.
3. To make the resources and wealth of Ireland subservient to the needs and welfare of all the people of Ireland.
4. To make Ireland, as far as possible, economically self-contained and self-sufficing.
5. To establish as many families as practicable on the land.
6. By suitable distribution of power to promote the ruralisation of industries essential to the lives of the people as opposed to their concentration in the cities.
7. To carry out the Democratic Programme of the First Dáil.

It can, of course be taken for granted that not all of the party, by any means, knew the details of the Democratic

Programme of the First Dáil and that some of those who did took it with a grain of salt. Nevertheless, it sounded well and as they were all at least Sinn Féiners, the policy that emerged from the interaction of the differing attitudes of individuals was definitely radical and orientated towards Aim No. 3, which it now appears is contrary to the 1937 Constitution — just as most of the others are over-ruled by EEC rules and regulations. It is probably true that virtually the entire original membership was sincere even about Aim No. 2 although, with some outstanding exceptions, the attitude was to encourage this by precept rather than by example. To the best of my knowledge this aim has not been amended even by substituting *a spoken language* for *the spoken language*. Still, although all efforts to get any significant Fianna Fáil input into the language movement have been complete failures (and there have been some such efforts), I remember the occasional incident which showed that there was in fact an amount of sincerity in regard to this aim even among members who were never more than *A Chairde Ghaeil* men.

An instance that springs to mind concerns a resolution calling for a reversal of the language policy, which some of the party's new acquisitions, known at the time as 'mohairs' (and sometimes as 'mohawks'), succeeded in getting on to the Ard Fheis Clár. I was contemplating the unusual step, for a member of the officer board, of getting in early on the debate to make it clear to these people that they were in the wrong party, when I discovered that this would not be necessary. Some of the older and most respected members, who had never been specifically identified as language enthusiasts, were incensed that such a resolution could have emanated from any unit of the Fianna Fáil organisation and they were lined up, headed by Dan Breen and Major de Valera, to mark the 'mohairs' card in no uncertain terms. In the event, the resolution was not reached; the National Executive gave it short shrift; and despite further infiltration by the quaintly misnamed Language Freedom Movement, it never re-surfaced up to the time I left. I recall also at the start of a general election campaign shortly after I became honorary secretary, I was reading through the usual circular summoning the constituency conventions to select candidates. This included the ritual admonition to delegates that, wherever possible, preference should be given to candidates with a sound knowledge of Irish. I remarked to the general secretary, Tomás Ó Maoláin, who himself was always ready and anxious to speak Irish at any time, that this was farcical and that, if anyone at all adverted to it, it would be treated as a joke and I asked was it not time we stopped making fools of ourselves? If we could not find a way of ensuring the availability of candidates with Irish, there was no point in trying to salve our consciences with this nonsense which impressed no one and would at best be ignored. He exploded and I got a ten minute lecture on what Fianna Fáil was all about. I knew what it was about all right but even at that stage, I was beginning to suspect a certain amount of hypocrisy. The admonition survived and I would not be surprised if it still survives to the present day when with a few exceptions almost all Fianna Fáil ministers and ministers-of-state appear to have no Irish at all and when a second Fianna Fáil Taoiseach appears to have let a once competent facility in the language deteriorate unnecessarily. Still, a number of incidents such as those I have mentioned suggested to me that there was also a great deal of sincerity about all of the seven aims. Unfortunately this was negatived by a great level of complacency and an almost absolute, child-like confidence in the top echelon of the party which by that time was fully occupied in the day-to-day administration of government. Policy emanated mainly from the civil service but was marginally adjusted by the cumulative effect, on individual ministers, of party opinion and of public opinion filtered by the party.

I remember getting an earlier demonstration of what Fianna Fáil meant both to its members and to the general public when the party was nearing and I was emerging from the teenage stage. This was in 1938 when I had the privilege of travelling on the special train bringing the invited guests from Dublin for the ceremonial handing over of the ports from British to Irish control at Spike Island. Thousands of people were gathered at Kingsbridge Station to cheer the ministers, deputies and other dignitaries as they arrived and as the train departed. Eventually the crowd realised there was something wrong and, feeling cheated, they began to call for de Valera but the former President of the Executive Council of the Irish Free State, newly designated Taoiseach na hÉireann had gone by road. Too late the other members of the government realised what a mistake this was and there was something approaching consternation until my father suggested that, since the new Liberator was not available in person 'we better give them the next best thing — Dan Breen'. Breen was persuaded to show himself at the window and immediately evoked the required effect, which even a mass appearance of the government had failed to produce. The platform erupted as the hill in Croke Park erupts when Dublin score a goal. The people had certainly got the next best thing. They were just as ambivalent as Fianna Fáil. They had come to cheer the completion of the achievement of Twenty-six County sovereignty by peaceful means but they were happy instead to pay homage to the physical force movement by cheering the living symbol of all the men of violence, who had made this day possible by adopting the only initiative which ever wrested any colonial possession from Britain's grasp, from the United States of America to Las Malvinas. And Fianna Fáil, who had not yet learned the new doctrine that 'history is bunk' and that, in fact, nothing was ever achieved by violence, gloated in the people's vociferous endorsement of their violent past and their current ambivalence. At every station along the line the pattern was the same — to the delight of the waiting crowds, Dan Breen, symbolising the violent Republican origin of Fianna Fáil, stood in for the absent Leader, who had tidied up the achievement of the men of violence. On the way back TDs, ministers and senators, veterans of 1916, the Black and Tan War and the Civil War, with the famed Tipperary trio of Breen, Seán Hayes and Bill Quirke prominent among them, were slapping one another on the back and saying, 'We won't have another drink until we get the Six Counties back'. Those were the days! I don't suppose there was anyone aboard who knew the dictionary definition of Republican, but they all knew their Aim No. 1. It was still an unsophisticated party — and an ignorant one that had to wait almost another thirty-five years to discover the meaning of its sub-title.

Other factors, mainly bread and butter matters, gradually began to take effect but it was the original basic aims that marked the party out as different, that gave it its character as the national movement rather than a mere political party, that sustained it with its morale intact through all vicissitudes and that gave it a collective will to win capable of overcoming even the personal cupidity of the latter-day intake of politicians on the make. This effect survived — for a time — the formal ratification by the 1971 Ard Fheis of the effective renunciation of Aim No. 1 *(See Appendix A, p. 140)*. Members who understood clearly exactly what had happened could not bring themselves to face the reality. They would take the option de Valera, as President of Sinn Féin, rejected in 1925; they would work from within. They could not and would not see that in a party where the prime principle was that the Leader must never be challenged, it was not possible to work from within. The thing to be worked against was fundamental and the only way to tackle it was to follow the 1925 precedent by a straightforward confrontation and by secession in the event of that failing. Either the policy on the Six Counties issue had been reversed or it had not — there were no two ways about it, and if it had been reversed, there was a vacuum requiring to be filled in constitutional politics just as there was when Sinn Féin decided not to alter the original post-Treaty decision to boycott the Dáil and not to recognise the institutions of the new Irish Free State. Throughout the whole of the 1970s I could scarcely walk a hundred yards in any town in Ireland without people stopping me to tell me they knew what I said was right but had thought it better to stay on because, as they put it, 'I couldn't let the Blueshirts back'. This was at a time when the Blueshirts had spent more than thirty years on the ashpit of history waiting for Ronald Reagan to dump the commies on top of them. For instance, I couldn't and still can't walk, however furtively, through Ballinasloe Fair without people from all over the west catching me by the sleeve to tell me they agreed with me but decided to stay inside and to this day, the car-park attendant at big Croke Park games will say, 'Jaysis, Kevin you should have stayed to help us'.

The folk memory of the La Scala meeting regarded as the climax of the Treaty split, the Civil War and the aftermath of repression, embodied as it is in the Seven Aims, delayed the inevitable deterioration in the quality of the Fianna Fáil organisation until the elected representatives themselves got the message and ousted their Leader — not on any matter of principle but solely to avoid what was seen as a threat to their own good jobs. Then the rot set in and now it appears every TD is a potential conspirator and defector always watching for the hop of the ball, to seize on what may be an opportunity for personal advancement and 'May the divil take the hindmost'.

5

What Decline?

This book purports to deal with the rise and decline of Fianna Fáil. The members of the party of pragmatism may very well ask, 'What decline?' They can point with conviction and confidence to the record of election results and say, 'We don't see any decline. We reached our potential as the majority in 1932, six years after our formation; we have retained that position comfortably at every election since; we have never at any stage during any count looked like losing it; and we don't look like losing it now. Since 1932, the total number of seats obtained by all other parties contesting the election has never exceeded our total. Our total has been equalled by the total of all other parties once only and this happened only because Neil Blaney was temporarily and marginally outside the party but in external association with it. Since and including 1932 there have been eighteen general elections; we have formed the government after all of those except five and we have never since 1932 been out of government for two successive periods. The results over the last half century prove that throughout that period the people have continuously realised that they need Fianna Fáil either as government or on hand to take over after they have indulged in the disastrous luxury of a government dominated by Fine Gael. . .'

The results of the elections since and including 1932 are shown opposite:

Year	Total of Seats	Government	Seats	Fianna Fáil % of Total	Cum. na. nG. or Fine Gael
1932	153	Fianna Fáil	72	47.06	57
1933	153	Fianna Fáil	77	50.33	48
1937	138	Fianna Fáil	69	50.00	48
1938	138	Fianna Fáil	77	55.79	45
1943	138	Fianna Fáil	67	48.55	32
1944	138	Fianna Fáil	76	55.07	30
1948	147	Coalition	68	46.26	31
1951	147	Fianna Fáil	69	46.94	40
1954	147	Coalition	65	44.22	50
1957	147	Fianna Fáil	78	53.06	40
1961	144	Fianna Fáil	70	48.61	47
1965	144	Fianna Fáil	72	50.00	47
1969	144	Fianna Fáil	75	52.08	50
1973	144	Coalition	69	47.91	54
1977	148	Fianna Fáil	84	56.76	43
1981	166	Coalition	78	46.99	65
1982	166	Fianna Fáil	81	48.79	63

It is as well to say at the outset that no manipulation of the electoral figures can show either an actual decline or signs of a decline to come in support for Fianna Fáil or in their prospects of maintaining their predominant position. Whatever signs there are of a future decline in the party's political fortunes are of a different nature and the actual decline I see is certainly of a different nature. I have given figures for the percentage of seats won because this is the actual result according to the rules of our electoral system, i.e. the system described for some reason as the Single Transferable Vote, operated in three seat, four seat and five seat constituencies, except for a short period in the early years of the State when there were some larger constituencies. There is no point in considering other factors lazily referred to as the vagaries of PR. These are part of the system. There are no vagaries of PR, which is an artificial system with rigid rules producing results solely in accordance with these rules. There may be vagaries by the voters but that is what democracy is all about. The percentage of first preference votes can only give a rough indication while *Magill's* new idea of the Last Effective Count is available only after the result and is not by any means accurate or consistently arrived at. The ultimate vote accredited by the complete working of the Single Transferable Vote system to party candidates is not, in fact, available in all constituencies because, of course, the count is carried out to its conclusion in some constituencies but in others the returning officer decides on the basis of the figures at the penultimate stage that the final result could not be affected by a further elimination or distribution of surplus. This is quite logical and fair but it means that the Last Effective Vote is not available according to the same standards in every constituency and some candidates are returned without reaching the quota, who might have a larger Last Effective Vote than some of those who are returned with a quota, if the full process had been carried out. To argue that an election was won or lost through the vagaries of PR is like a GAA team claiming a moral victory because they had more of the play but their forwards shot too many wides, when the only relevant consideration is that one goal equals three points and that wides equal nothing, or like a member of a past rugby team arguing that if the value of a try had always been as it is now the result of a particular match would have been different. The fact is that our elections are decided not on the basis of first preference votes but on the interpretation of these votes by the arbitrary rules of the Single Transferable Vote.

This system has invariably worked in Fianna Fáil's favour to some degree. The excess of the percentage of seats over the percentage of votes has varied between the limits of 6.65 in 1943 to 0.61 in 1951. In the record majority year of 1977 the figure for this excess of seats over votes was 6.16. In that year the figure for the first preference votes was not, in fact, a record. This figure for PR advantage, which is undetectable at any stage of the count until the end, is the critical factor, which makes the forecasting of the ultimate result on the basis of first preference swings merely a game of chance. The fact that this is so is not a vagary of PR. It is an essential feature of PR. When the percentage swing is known, it is necessary in order to make a credible forecast to know also this PR advantage and this emerges only when the count is over and by that time the computer has invariably made a fool of itself. On the basis of past results it is necessary to add some figure, which up to now has been between 6.65 and 0.61 to the Fianna Fáil percentage vote in order to arrive at the result. One can take the average of these figures over the years to make a guess but there is always the possibility that at some election these limits will be extended. There is no reason why it should not go up to ten or why it should not at some election become a negative factor. Recent election results have not indicated a downward trend in the advantage Fianna Fáil obtains from the electoral system. It may be that current public opinion indicates the likelihood of a significant change but there are no figures of actual results to show this. To make an educated guess at the actual outcome of an election after the first count results are available it is necessary to make an assessment of each individual constituency based on local knowledge. This is a job for active party politicians, not academic statisticians and, while a computer may have an unerring mechanical brain it has no common sense. (A computer on the public sector pay roll recently sent me a Final Demand for an overdue account of £0.00.) There is no pattern in the relationship between the PR advantage and the percentage first preference votes. Low votes have coincided with both high and low PR advantages and the same applies in the case of high votes. I have not gone to the trouble of adjusting the various figures to take account of the fact that the Ceann Comhairle is returned automatically because it does not matter. The only relevant thing is the result and the results to date show no deterioration in the electoral performance of Fianna Fáil.

In fact the results show a remarkable similarity in the pattern of the first twenty-five years since 1932 and the second such period, which has just ended. Fianna Fáil's first period of office lasted for sixteen years from 1932 to 1948. This was followed by a nine year period when Fianna Fáil alternated with a Coalition government from 1948 to 1957. When Fianna Fáil got back in 1957 they remained for another sixteen years and this has again been followed by a nine year period of alternating Fianna Fáil and Coalition governments. There were, of course, some differences in the two twenty-five year periods. For instance, in the first sixteen years of Fianna Fáil government there were seven general elections in six of which they were successful and one in which they were defeated. In the second sixteen year period there were only five general elections, four successful and one unsuccessful. In the first nine year period each Coalition government lasted approximately three years while, in the second, one lasted four years and the other lasted one year. Some people may find it of interest to note that Fianna Fáil's first sixteen year period of office commenced nine years after the first post-Treaty elections in 1923, so that it could be said that there has been a recurring nine, sixteen pattern since the foundation of the State. I gather that there would not be many who would bet on this as an indication that the accession to government of Fianna Fáil in March 1982 initiated another unbroken period, which will not end until the second centenary of 1798. It appears that by that time we'll all fear to speak of '98. Certainly programme presenters in RTE will. The question now is: 'Are Fianna Fáil starting another long period of government or is the pattern to be broken?' This is for the future to decide but, contrary to the general impression created by the media political correspondents who are the acknowledged experts, the fact is that in the 1973-82 period, Fianna Fáil's electoral fortunes have not sunk anywhere nearly as low as in the earlier 'see-saw' period of 1948-57. The relevant figures for the percentage of seats are:

1948	46.26%	Coalition government
1951	46.94%	Fianna Fáil government
1954	44.22%	Coalition government
1957	53.06%	Fianna Fáil government

and in the second period:

1973	47.91%	Coalition government
1977	56.76%	Fianna Fáil government
1981	46.99%	Coalition government
1982	48.79%	Fianna Fáil government

The 1954 figure is, in fact, the lowest level of seats achieved by Fianna Fáil since 1927 and the figure for 1981, which resulted in a Coalition government, was virtually the same as that which produced a Fianna Fáil government in 1951. In 1951 this was sufficient to maintain Fianna Fáil in government for three years while in 1981 it was sufficient to limit the life of the Coalition government to eight months. Their numerical position in the Dáil at the end of this nine year period is, however, considerably worse than it was in 1957. This may be significant although it can be pointed out that they are marginally better than in 1932, when an early general election stabilised their position. Many people believe there will be an early election this time also but times are different and it is by no means sure this would produce the same result as in 1933. It can also be pointed out that, while the fall in the percentage of seats from one election to another was greatest in 1981 at 9.77 as against 8.81 in 1948, it fell from a higher figure, the result therefore being marginally better from the party's point of view than in 1948, that recovery has been more rapid so far, and that the Coalition government formed in 1981 lasted only a few months as against three years in the case of the 1948 Coalition. The position still is that in eighteen general elections in the last fifty years Fianna Fáil have won thirteen and been ousted in five, each time by a Coalition. In that fifty year period no government other than Fianna Fáil has been in office for as much as two successive periods, however short, and this is the real test. To gain office is one thing, to retain it is another. So far no Coalition, under three different Taoisigh, has succeeded in doing this and the last Coalition established a record for the shortest period in government since the foundation of the State. This means, in effect, that the record to date appears to show that the Fine Gael-Labour Coalition has not got the capacity to provide a period of stable government even when Fianna Fáil are in disarray. Normally a government gaining office has had the advantage of being able to capitalise on the unpopular things every government has to do and on every adversity that has affected any section of the community, while a government retaining office has had to overcome the effects of these things. Obviously, it becomes even more of an achievement to retain government for a third period and still more for a fourth, fifth and sixth as Fianna Fáil has done and, conversely, it is easier to defeat a government, which has been in office for sixteen years than one which is still only running itself in. Fianna Fáil's record is to have retained office in no less than eight general elections out of eighteen and always to have regained office after one period in opposition. So they still have this unbroken tradition behind them starting the fifty-first year since coming to power. It is something like the tradition from which a Kerry football team starts the championship campaign.

On figures, on patterns, on trends and on tradition, then, there is no reason to assert there is a Fianna Fáil electoral decline or to forecast that there is one on the way. There are, however, other kinds of decline and there are considerations other than figures. The most relevant circumstance leading to the fairly general belief that the ending of the second nine year see-saw period will not mark the beginning of another extended period of Fianna Fáil government is that, for the first time ever, there is in each constituency, to the knowledge of the whole electorate, a faction bitterly opposed to the leadership and that in some cases this is the majority faction. This is a symptom of a complete metamorphosis of the party, a process that has been a long time in gestation, the development of which has been apparent to anyone who knew the basic principles from which the Fianna Fáil ethos grew but which to the extraneous, objective, academic but uninitiated observer appears to have come suddenly. So now the experts say there is a decline in Fianna Fáil irrespective of what the figures say. Since there is such an obvious deterioration in quality, in mutual loyalty, in unity of purpose, in morale and in the capacity to adopt and pursue a coherent and consistent approach to political problems, it is assumed that erosion of electoral support will be of corresponding proportions. There are other factors to be considered before coming to this conclusion but maybe the experts are right. Who am I to contradict them? They must get it right some time. Whether the electoral collapse comes sooner or later, the probability is that everyone cannot be wrong. Every other conceivable aspect of decline is clearly there and the only question is 'When did what appeared to be, according to how one looked at it, either a continuing rise or a position of unshakeable stability become a headlong decline?'

6

Hurrah! Hurrah!
We Bring the Jubilee

If I am right in saying that it is more difficult to retain power as government in a general election than it is to get into power by defeating the existing government, then Fianna Fáil's stature as a political party has been continuously rising. Certainly, the record of the first twenty-five years gave every reason for the triumphalist celebration of the Silver Jubilee. First came the meteoric rise from its origin as the second Sinn Féin splinter party to the government of the Irish Free State in a mere six years. In 1932 Fianna Fáil became the government with 47.06% of the seats and a fifteen seat majority over the founders of the State. In 1933 this position was spectacularly improved with 50.33% of the seats and a majority of twenty-nine over Cumann na nGaedheal. A peculiar feature of the first sixteen years of Fianna Fáil government was that it took two elections each time to establish a satisfactory Dáil situation. The 1932/33 operation yielded 50.33% of the seats, which just sufficed. In 1937/38 the result was 55.79% of the seats and thirty-two seats more than Fine Gael, as they had become, and 1943/44 produced almost the same percentage of seats (55.07%) and forty-six more than Fine Gael. It almost appeared that, under the electoral system, the people needed a second look at what their initial reaction to the outgoing government's performance had produced, in order to carry out their real intentions. It certainly seems to substantiate the contention in the first sentence above as on these three successive occasions the electorate almost produced a result which they quickly saw as undesirable. 1937 and 1943 showed that the spontaneous reaction to a government's performance may be so adverse as to produce a change of government by accident. 1938 and 1944 showed that whatever hardship and personal frustration people had experienced they still wanted a Fianna Fáil government at least in preference to Fine Gael, who were still regarded as Blueshirts. Considering the difficult times throughout the whole of this period and the many necessarily unpopular decisions by the government, this was not merely standing still at the top; it demonstrated massive public confidence that could only have been achieved by decisive and responsible government following a clearly defined path. In 1948 the post-war reaction, which ousted Churchill, who brought the British through the war to victory, also defeated de Valera, who saved Ireland from the horrors of war. The defeat was of such a marginal nature that it appeared as if the people had made the mistake they nearly made in 1932 and 1943 and that they would rectify it if they got the chance, as they did in 1938 and 1944. By the time of the Jubilee, however, Fianna Fáil were back albeit in a numerical position almost identical with that which had proved inadequate in 1932 and this nine year indeterminate period eventually ended in 1957 with Fianna Fáil once more firmly in the saddle having obtained 53.06% of the seats and thirty-eight more than Fine Gael, despite the transfusions the latter party had received from the minor Coalition groups. It certainly could be convincingly and confidently proclaimed that the first twenty-five years of Fianna Fáil was a period of continuous success and no one could accuse them of failing to make this point in celebrating the occasion. Even the 1948 defeat was merely a hiccup produced by post-war hysteria and the result could not have been foreseen nor intended. Already in 1951 it appeared that the Coalition had been identified as unauthorised interlopers and that Fianna Fáil had again been given the authority to get on with the job.

This was surely the period of the young man's march on the line of national advance. The path mapped out in the La Scala in 1926 had been followed without deviation and with complete success. The position had been obtained where the solution of the final problem could be confidently undertaken. Sovereignty had been achieved and the fact of this sovereignty had been established before the world by the declaration and maintenance of neutrality in the war. Apart altogether from the listed achievements this real sovereignty had been made possible by the building of an economic basis which made a separate existence possible, and, while this applied only to the area of the Irish Free State, the Twenty-six County government had been able to prevent conscription in the Six Counties at the height of Britain's difficulties. So morale was high and the Republican motivation seemed to be as strong and as relevant as ever to the organisation as a whole, to the parliamentary party, to the members of the government, and in particular to the Taoiseach, who availed of the opportunity provided by his temporary release from the duties of Taoiseach in 1948 to tour the world enlisting the support of people of Irish descent for the confident undertaking of the solution of 'the problem of successfully bringing in the North'.

The unshakeable allegiance of the Fianna Fáil organisation throughout this period, when it was severely tested in every possible way, can be explained only by its total dedication to the national aim of securing the unity of the country as a Republic. This is what made it invincible and immune to the effects of personal hardship arising from government policy, which would erode the loyalty of a less idealistic party. For instance, the period 1932 to 1937 was the period of the economic war, when Britain, still a great imperial power, decided to crush the national advance and sad to say this was assisted by the Fine Gael party. The amazing steadfastness of the rural organisation, in particular, in all the vicissitudes of the economic war, was a truly outstanding example of absolute dedication to the national ideal without thought of self-interest An organisation composed entirely of small farmers stood firm as a rock while their calves were slaughtered and the already low standard of living of their families was further reduced. The widespread hardship was the direct result of Fianna Fáil's march on the line of national advance. A party bidding to oust the government could not have asked for more favourable conditions and Fine Gael, the new manifestation of Cumann na nGaedheal, had told the people in advance what to expect from the Fianna Fáil madness in reneging on the sanctified Treaty. In spite of this, so effective was the rural organisation and so impressive was their national enthusiasm that the voters also stood firm against the British economic bludgeon. The erosion of support between 1933 and 1937 was from 50.33% of the seats to exactly 50%, including the Ceann Comhairle, and in less than twelve months the people came to appreciate the great advance towards real nationhood effected by the New Constitution and, in a reaction to this and to the euphoria of the final British departure from the Twenty-six Counties, they gave Fianna Fáil the greatest percentage vote that has ever been achieved, and 55.79% of the seats. The people exercised their prerogative of grumbling in 1937 and then, in 1938, weighed their own sufferings—and they really did suffer—against the national gain and decided it was worth the sacrifice. In the province of Connaught, which was most severely affected by the hardships of the economic war, Fianna Fáil got exactly two-thirds of the seats. The contrast now, when no section of the people is prepared to make any sacrifice whatever for any purpose whatever, is not due to a deterioration in the calibre of the people; it is entirely due to the degeneration of the Fianna Fáil party and the consequent demoralisation of the membership. There is now no question of any political party providing national leadership. All that are available have been assessed on performance and found wanting. The public view of politicians is almost universally cynical and votes are for auction to be purchased by disastrous recklessness such as the 1977 Manifesto and by scandalous nonsensical bribes like Knock airport. In 1938 it was different — 'Yes, our calves were slaughtered, our produce in general had virtually to be given away and we had to stand by and see our families suffering. All this which the Opposition tell us is true, but the Oath of Allegiance is gone, the Governor-General is gone, the imposed Constitution is gone, the endorsement of the Boundary Agreement has been rescinded, the Ports are back and the Land Annuities, which we must still pay, remain on this side of the Irish Sea. The government has served us well.' The people of the disadvantaged areas along the west coast and contiguous areas stretching as far east as Monaghan, laughed at jokes about Mr de Valera's reply to the man breaking stones at the side of the road, 'It doesn't matter who gets in, you will still be breaking stones', and about the Kerry boatman who explained to his English patron that the reason Fianna Fáil got back into power was 'that poor people always vote for them and now there are more poor people that ever before'. They laughed and dug their heels in for the final phase of the national advance.

The economic war was followed by the wartime emergency, when all sections of the community suffered the effects of a small comparatively undeveloped State being suddenly thrown on its own resources. In spite of an unprecedented, comprehensive and still unequalled attempt to exploit the difficulties of the situation in the 1943 election, the people stood firm. The organisation understood exactly what was happening and, under attack from all sides by sectional interests, monetary reform theorists, the 'England's difficulty is Ireland's opportunity' brand of Republicanism, and Independents of all sorts, they succeeded in explaining it to the people. We were asserting our newly won sovereignty. We were undertaking the immense task of bringing the country, Thirty-two Counties, safely through a war in which we were equipped to play no role other than that of cannon fodder for the great powers. Nevertheless, this was the first election in which Fianna Fáil really experienced the effects of out-raged sectional interests. A proportion of the small farmers who had unitedly and heroically borne the brunt of the economic war rebelled against the war emergency measure of compulsory tillage, which was agricultural heresy to them, and as the large farmers had, in the main, always opposed Republicanism, the 1943 election produced the upsurge of Clann na Talmhan and the election of some independent farmer candidates. Still the actual erosion of support as measured by the Single Transferable Vote was marginal. Fianna Fáil's percentage of seats at 48.55 was marginally below an overall majority and the party con-tinued in office having, obviously, not been defeated by the people. Again within less than a year, the redoubled efforts of the organisation rallied support and stability was restored with 55.07% of the seats and again the support was rallied on the national issue of sovereignty against sectional interests. I remember that the slogan on which the election was fought and won remained painted in huge white lettering on the new sea-wall at Clontarf until, many years later, a Dutch engineering firm pumped sludge from Dublin Bay over the wall to form the new promenade, perhaps a sign of things to come. The slogan was *Stand by Dev and Safeguard the Nation.*

Although Fianna Fáil had its support, as measured by the electoral system, restored almost to the 1938 level, it was a significant fact that the compulsory tillage defections were never fully recovered. A section of the small farmers, the backbone of the Fianna Fáil party had broken ranks and, coming as it did in a time of national emergency, it was seen as a transfer of allegiance for personal reasons to the distrusted and disliked Fine Gael party, or Blueshirts as they were commonly referred to at the time. In the west, particularly the bitterness was on a scale approaching the post-Civil War situation and, sure enough, the disaffected small farmers' party went on to join with the new Clann na Poblachta party in letting Fine Gael back into office as the main partner of the Coalition in 1948, and over the years before it finally disappeared it gave Fine Gael a life-saving transfusion of Fianna Fáil foundation stock. In 1944, however, Fianna Fáil's overall support was restored and all seemed well but, in fact, the first breach in the solidarity of the forces which set out in 1926 on the national advance was not really healed. To a certain extent the continuing high level of support resulted from the replacement of the lost support rather than from its recovery.

In 1948, the nation had been satisfactorily safeguarded and we were out of the wood and could relax in the luxury of letting Fianna Fáil know that they had not a God-given mandate as the permanent government. The general election, giving Fianna Fáil only 46.26% of the seats, produced the most indecisive result since 1932. This was the cumulative effect of all the hardship and frustration of the economic war and the war-time emergency, the major factors being compulsory tillage and the shortage of tea, combined with a Republican backlash, arising from the repression of the militant Republican movement in the World War period, which was delayed until the war was over. This Republican backlash was marshalled by the new Clann na Poblachta party, which came into constitutional politics on the basis of the acceptance of the 1937 Constitution but won its support largely on the basis of opposition to the outlawing of militant opposition to the Constitutional position. It was a remarkable indication of the solidarity of the party and of the people's high opinion of it, that all this, with the added disadvantage of having been in office for sixteen continuous, difficult years and with the general post-war trend, left Fianna Fáil's Dáil strength reduced by only 0.8% from the level achieved when they first came to office in 1932. They still had one seat more than the combined strength of all the other parties but this time there were twelve Independents. Such a situation had always produced a Fianna Fáil minority government in the past. This seemed to be in accordance with the principles of democracy and on each previous occasion the people had said within twelve months that they did not mean to create a period of instabilty. There was no reason to expect that such a diversely composed opposition would attempt to coalesce to keep Fianna Fáil out but, on this occasion, neither the groups opposed to Fianna Fáil and to one another nor the assorted Independents were going to give Fianna Fáil another chance to redress the indecisive situation by a quick election. So, the impossible happened. To the general amazement of the people the unlikely Coalition of opposites was formed. Free Staters, Redmondites, extreme Republicans, Big and Small Farmers, Conservatives, Monetary Reformers, Socialist and non-Socialist Labour all joined together, but surely only temporarily to avert the established Fianna Fáil tactic of submitting the indecisive result to the electorate for a second opinion? It was merely a question of how long they could exist in Coalition, a question of whether the Coalition's lifetime would be measured in weeks or months. In fact, the first Coalition government lasted for three years and the coalition arrangement has lasted ever since in government and opposition with Fine Gael subsuming all its partners until only a weakened and sickly Labour party remains. Fianna Fáil's basic Republican allegiance was the factor which virtually welded the organisation together and made it invincible, and it was this invincibility in turn which cemented the fundamentally unstable Coalition together. It is only now when the Republican allegiance has lost its grip and been replaced by selfish materialism that the aura of invincibilty has weakened. As a direct result, the Coalition is showing signs of breaking up and Fine Gael is, for the first time since it emerged from the ashes of Cumann na nGaedheal, actually showing signs of developing the confidence to go it alone.

In 1951, however, Fianna Fáil were back and, as the presumptuous alternative appeared to have been disposed of, the Jubliee clebrations were uninhibited. The Capitol (La Scala) concert ended with the ringing tones of the celebrated tenor, Frank Ryan, singing *The Bold Fenian Men*. Rededicated to its original programme, revivified by de Valera's inspiring rhetoric, Fianna Fáil started out on the second twenty-five years to the tune of 'Out and make way for the Bold Fenian Men'. Just as O'Connell's followers accepted without question that 1843 would be 'Repeal Year', so the Soldiers of Destiny accepted that they were about to take the final step back to the Republic. It is true that the Coalition had declared the Twenty-six County State to be a Republic but this was regarded as a sacriligious misappropriation of a title which could legitimately be applied only to the Thirty-two Counties. The time had now come when the Soldiers of the Legion of the Rearguard were once more to take their place with the Vanguard, this time without actual recourse to arms. The remainder of the course had been mapped out by Mr de Valera's world tour during the Coalition inter regnum 'The gravest injury one nation could inflict upon another' must be rectified where the crime was perpetrated in the British parliament. From the hallowed 1926 stage they were given their marching orders for the final phase of the advance. Their morale as the Fianna Fáil party was as high as it had ever been. The Republican ethos appeared to be intact having survived twenty-five years almost all in the Free State Assembly. There was no apparent evidence of incipient decline. The young men were still on the march and, believing the ultimate objective was now in sight, no one noticed creaking joints or fallen arches. If there was deviation or a tendency to deviate, the rank and file knew nothing of it. There were, however, two significant things which were not apparent: the failure to attach any real significance to the belated conversion of Fine Gael or to consolidate that conversion so as to unite the national forces and mobilise them for the solution of the problem, and secondly, the self-seeking materialists or 'mohairs' were arriving on the scene.

By this time the list of Fianna Fáil's achievements, which had cleared the way for the final step, had become the most widely known and most frequently heard recitation in Ireland. Every member of every cumann throughout the Twenty-six Counties could repeat it without fault at a moment's notice and, liberally interspersed with reverential references to Eamon de Valera, it served as the framework of Dáil and county council election speeches at every chapel gate and market square throughout the State. The record certainly showed unremitting adherence to the pursuit of the basic objective of the party and, Clann na Poblachta notwithstanding, no one saw the slightest indication of any weakening of the Republican resolve.

Many years later, the supine reaction of the government in 1969-70 and the subsequent development to full-scale participation in the British effort to impose a military solution in the Six Counties consolidating Partition prompted me to scan the past for signs that should have been seen, and it was only then I realised the first twenty-five years of Republican achievement had also shown this degree of insincerity. In the La Scala, de Valera had said:

> Can the people be brought together again for a great national advance? Merely to shout unity will not, we know, be enough. An adequate national policy must be found. Cut in two as the national forces are now — one section pulling one way and the other the opposite way — it is vain to

expect progress. The imperial forces are certain of easy triumph. They defeat one section of nationalism within the Free State assembly. Then they combine with that section to defeat us — the other section — outside. Victory for nationalism cannot come like that. Means must be found to bring the national forces together — together at least to this extent — that the two sections will, in the main, proceed along parallel lines and in a common direction, so that the resultant of their combined efforts may be the greatest possible.

As I have pointed out in Chapter One, this position had been achieved and this was the critical factor which created the position 'in which the solution of the problem of successfully bringing in the North, could be confidently undertaken.' Surely this was not the least of Fianna Fáil's achievements? The section of nationalism, defeated within the Free State assembly, had been redeemed in the new situation resulting from Fianna Fáil's constitutional achievements. It was the creation of this new situation that produced Clann na Poblachta and this new party proved to be the catalyst which brought the national forces together for a brief but solemn joint declaration of national policy. This was the culmination of the first twenty-five years but the Fianna Fáil litany ended with the 1939-45 declaration and maintenance of neutrality. Why was this? Was it because the unanimous Dáil Resolution setting out the national position and formalising this bringing of the national forces together was proposed by the leader of the section defeated within the Free State assembly and only seconded by de Valera? Or was it that Republicanism had become the cherished possession of the Fianna Fáil party, not to be shared with outsiders? Had the aim, 'To secure the Unity and Independence of Ireland as a Republic' become so important as an aim in itself that it was seen as a necessary permanent feature of Fianna Fáil?

When Fianna Fáil were out of office for the first time since 1932, the party leader, former Taoiseach of Ireland and former President of the Irish Republic, undertook a world tour totally related to the solution of the final problem in the only way it could be ended, i.e. by the ending of the injustice done to the Irish nation by the nation which perpetrated the injustice in the first place and was continuing to perpetrate it. Is there any explanation for the decision to undertake such a major operation other than that this was regarded as a matter of the greatest urgency? How then could there have been an almost simultaneous decision not to avail of the resultant of the two sections of the national forces acting in a solemnly specified common direction which was decided after long and detailed consultation between the two sections? Would not the sense of urgency which had led to the world tour also have dictated the employment of the combined effort of the two sections of the national forces, whose colours were now, with great pomp and ceremony, nailed to the same mast? There are cynics who suggest that the only reasonable explanation is that the highly publicised tour was related to the need to get the Fianna Fáil party back into power rather than to the accomplishment of the aim which, if achieved, would make the sub-title 'Republican Party' obsolete.

In any case, the rotation of Fine Gael policy to a direction parallel to Fianna Fáil's was not mentioned in any of the Jubilee literature; it never became part of the basic Fianna Fáil election speech; the 'resultant of their combined efforts' was not applied to the task of moving the British resistance as was envisaged in 1926; it was ignored and, not surprisingly, when the Clann na Poblachta catalyst disappeared, Fine Gael policy swung back to its original direction; and, in 1970, Fianna Fáil policy under the weight of accumulated Free State fat took up a position parallel to and in the same direction as Fine Gael's. During the brief period with the two sections of the national forces proceeding along parallel lines and in a common direction towards the achievement of the national aim, the idea of using the resultant for the purpose postulated in 1926 was rejected. Now some twenty years later they were again proceeding along parallel lines in a common direction and by standing up and deciding that the 1920 solution must end, the third section of the national forces, which was in the terms of the Constitution 'pending re-integration', ensured that this time the resultant of the two Twenty-six County sections must come into play. The tragedy was that now the common direction was towards maintaining the *status quo* and the result of this was that the Provisional IRA was virtually conjured into existence as the only force available to promote the officially unanimously adopted national aim. They did this with the aim stated in a slightly less uncompromising and more thoughtful form than the unanimous resolution of the constitutional politicians in Dáil Éireann, which has never been rescinded or amended. When, eventually, the inexorable post-war process of the de-imperialisation of Britain produces the end of the always resisted British dimension in Ireland, history must record that this result was the achievement of the men of violence even though the professional politicians may succeed in jumping on the band wagon in time for the grand finale and the applause.

My father always ascribed the beginning of the degeneration of Fianna Fáil to the receipt and acceptance of the first big money subscription. The third aim in the party constitution was 'To make the resources and wealth of Ireland subservient to the needs and welfare of all the people of Ireland', and, while the party never regarded itself as socialist, this was seriously intended and generally accepted as the underlying principle of its economic policy. There was no written commitment to keep aloof from the financial and commercial establishment but, in the beginning, everyone understood this to be the natural and essential policy. Economic development would produce and indeed require the development of an entrepreneurial and profit-making class. It would be too much to say that this was seen almost as a necessary evil but Republican policy always envisaged that personal wealth would be of more modest proportions than in the already developed countries. It was implicit in Aim No. 3, not to mention the Programme of the First Dáil. My father was one of those who always saw it as essential that the big business elements which were, of course, very important, should be kept strictly to their own milieu. It was always obvious to him that a party could imperceptibly lose a certain amount of its independence if a comparatively small number of individual subscriptions comprised a significant part of total income. His attitude must have rubbed off on me to a certain extent because, without ever making a specific decision, I always regarded it as important not to foregather with the princes of commerce to the extent that one might be in danger of coming to identify their interests with the national interest. It was all right to mix and be friendly with them when the occasion arose but it was important to keep them at arm's length and, after each such instance of high-level socialising, to remember to rehabilitate oneself by contact with the real, live Fianna Fáil organisation. This was essential to keep one's feet on the ground. The business moguls had their function which was an important one, but Fianna Fáil's function was different. I could see that Seán Lemass was right about the need for merchant adventurers, but it was important to remember they were a means not an end. Their success was not begrudged but it was a mere by-product of national policy. Another example of ambivalence I suppose some people would say.

When, in the early thirties, a subscription of the un-dreamed-of amount of £500 from the late Mr Joe McGrath arrived without warning at the party headquarters, the general secretary immediately realised that, apart from the fact that Mr McGrath was a well known supporter and financial backer of Cumann na nGaedheal, this would run counter to the Fianna Fáil ethos. He showed the letter to my father who, as one of the joint honorary secretaries, always kept in touch with headquarters which he tried to visit daily. He asked, 'What am I going to do about this?' The reply was immediate and as he expected, 'Send it back to him, of course.' It was sent back by return of post, with the polite explanation that it was party policy not to accept subscriptions of this nature. Mr Lemass, who was the other joint honorary secretary, raised the matter at a subsequent meeting either of the National Executive or the Officer Board and the result of the discussion was a decision to accept the subscription. It should be understood that there was no suggestion of any unworthy motive on Mr McGrath's part in this matter nor, indeed, any implication by him that his basic pro-Treaty attitude had changed. He was one of the comparatively few pro-Treaty people who, in spite of the bitter conflict, succeeded in retaining their original principles and regard for those who continued to adhere to the Republic. His personal friendship with Mr Lemass, who was a Civil War opponent, was genuine and by no means unique on Mr McGrath's part. Many of the Republicans most active in the Civil War, realising that they were marked men after the cease-fire, had no option but to emigrate to the United States and Canada and it is generally accepted that it was from these the agents for the Irish Hospitals Sweepstakes were recruited by Mr McGrath's own decision. It was largely through their efforts the undertaking was so successful and this, in turn, helped them to acquire a good standard of living in their new surroundings. Everyone knew this. The objection was to the principle of accepting big subscriptions from financial interests.

My father could see the gradual change in character from then on and watched futilely while it developed. This incident combined with his contention that industrial development should as far as possible be based on the utilisation of our own resources and his caustic comments on industries such as the car assembly industry, which he regarded as lunacy, was the start of a limited degree of antagonism between himself and Mr Lemass. Mr Lemass regarded him as a myopic Sinn Féiner who did not appreciate the difference between opposition and government, while my father regarded many of the industries developed behind a protective tariff wall as nonsense, since they could never hope to compete in quality or in price with the British products which they were copying. His idea was that an all-out development of those industries which used native raw materials and which did not depend entirely on expertise not available at home was the proper policy.

The acceptance of this subscription was a major decision, which, I suppose, helped the development of the party — it certainly made decisions to call general elections easier — but it was a new beginning and, certainly, not all the party realised the dangers involved to fundamental principles. It is, at least, an arguable proposition that this decision contained within it the seeds of the parasitic growth which eroded the Fianna Fáil ethos and eventually produced the Parliamentary Party so starkly exposed to the view of a shocked public after the 1982 general election.

7

What Jubilee?

As events turned out, Fianna Fáil had not disposed of the
new challenge to their supremacy in 1951. The people
needed a further experience of the Coalition to really get it
out of their system. The first Coalition government ended
in the 'mother and child' debacle and the second ended in
March 1957 with the unemployed sitting on O'Connell
Bridge. This time the nine years period of indecision was
over. There was no alternative to Fianna Fáil and the first
national aim could be, and was, put into cold storage. Mr
de Valera's world tour played its part in the 1951 election
but that was the last time the solution of the final problem
entered into an election campaign until during the 1973-77
Coalition certain elements in Fianna Fáil, searching for the
reason for their defeat and the road back, decided that
electoral tactics if not party strategy required a formal return to traditional party policy whether the Taoiseach and
his adherents liked it or not. Unlike the governments of
1932, 1937 and 1943, the Fianna Fáil minority government
formed in 1951 did not opt for an early general election but
continued in office until 1954. Then the people voted fairly
definitely to give the Coalition another chance, giving
Fianna Fáil only 44.22% of the seats — the lowest support
to the present date ever received by the party since before
1932, as measured by the distillation of the votes through
the process of the Single Transferable Vote. The result of
giving the Coalition the second bite at the cherry was that,
in 1957, the only argument required was that the Coalition
had wrecked the economy not once but twice and that this
was, obviously, the inevitable outcome of a Coalition of
opposites, which was the only alternative to Fianna Fáil. It
was a plausible argument and the unemployed were there
on O'Connell Bridge to prove it. At 53.06% the distilled
support for Fianna Fáil was satisfactory and little more was

necessary than the effective contrasting of the results of stable and decisive Fianna Fáil government with those of unstable Coalition government for Fianna Fáil to stay in power through the 1961, 1965 and 1969 elections. Measured electorally, this was another period of continuous rise for Fianna Fáil following the nine year period of public indecision from 1948 to 1957. They were returned to power in four successive general elections covering a period of sixteen years and, as I have pointed out before, that was a continuous rise in political fortunes and showed they were not merely standing still at the top. The latest menace, the influx into the Labour party of television and other prestigious academics, whose supposed aim was to make the seventies socialist, was ignominiously defeated in 1969 and with 52.08% Dáil representation, Fianna Fáil were firmly established for a further period of overall dominance. There was not a sign of a serious challenge. Morale had never been higher: our enemies were confounded, a footstool under our feet and we were invincible again.

The changes in the character of the party and, most significant of all, the change in motivation which had come about, were to the best of my knowledge not appreciated by the membership at any level, with two exceptions — Neil Blaney and myself. I had been worried for some time, indeed almost from the time I became a member of the government in 1957, and I was fully alerted to the degeneration of the Republican ethos of the party by the interim Report of the Colley Committee on the Constitution published in December 1967. From at least the time the preliminary Civil Rights rumblings started in the Six Counties, Blaney began to make a nuisance of himself by introducing the extraneous matter of the Six Counties into government meetings concerned with the full time job of consolidating the party's position of pre-eminence. He insisted on warning us, reasonably accurately as events turned out, of the troubles to come. He warned of the danger and the opportunity but was regarded as a persistent and disruptive Cassandra. The government stuck manfully to the task of minding its own business throughout the period marked in the Six Counties by Paisley's increasingly strident rantings.

and terrorist threats, by the founding of the Civil Rights
Association in 1967, by the breaking up of the Civil Rights
march in Derry by the RUC in October 1968, by Burntollet
and the enforced resignation of Captain O'Neill by
Loyalist bombings, and by the Apprentice Boys' march in
Derry followed by the siege of the Bogside on 12 August
1969 in the middle of the Irish government's summer holi-
days. By this time, without having the same personal knowledge of the situation on the ground but with virtually in-
bred knowledge that this was what Fianna Fáil had been
waiting for since 1926 and, more specifically, since 1951, I
was almost as troublesome as Blaney. The bogside erup-
tion immediately produced Haughey as the third member
of a Caucus which insisted this was our business, the
moment of truth for the Fianna Fáil party, the time for the
solution of the final problem, the time for which we the
then government had been waiting so very patiently since
1957. From the very beginning the reaction of the government was one of shock — even to me, and I was probably
the only member who had read the Report of the Committee on the Constitution, which could well have been produced by the old Cumann na nGaedheal party headquarters in 1937, without any assistance from the new
breed of new young men who represented Fianna Fáil on
the Committee.

After the ritual renewal of the baptismal vows in the
Capitol Theatre in 1951 the march on the line of national
advance had gradually ground to a halt. Possibly the troops
were entitled to a rest before re-grouping for the final stage
but the fall-out lasted for an extended period. In August
1969 it was clear that the time to fall in had arrived but
there was no one to give the order and the swinging stride
of the first twenty-five years was not forthcoming. I suppose an eighteen year fall-out was a bit excessive. The
highly publicised, continuing and escalating travail of the
section of the national majority coerced into the United
Kingdom, ensured that the matter of the basic reason for
the existence of the party could no longer be dismissed as
being currently irrelevant. In the La Scala Mr de Valera
had said:

We must, if we really want to succeed, endeavour to judge the situation just as it is, measure our strength against it, lay our plans and then act with courage and tenacity.

All these things the leadership was determined not to do and, above all, there was going to be no question of acting with courage and tenacity. There were some vague and scattered rumblings in the organisation but there was no ground swell and, since the leadership reacted only to ground swells, there was no resumption of the march. The most the Cabinet Caucus could achieve was an extended Mark Time period which lasted until May 1970. Then the Caucus was suddenly and dramatically eliminated in the courageous, tenacious and carefully engineered action of the Arms Non-Crisis.

The Citizens Defence Committees were carefully led up the garden path and delivered to their enemies. The pattern of events in the Six Counties for the past twelve years was decided by the Fianna Fáil government who abdicated the leadership of the national cause to which they had been dedicated at birth and handed it over to the Provisional IRA. From then on policy was unequivocal and it was the reverse of the line of national advance. It had been adumbrated succinctly a number of times at government meetings during the brief existence of the Caucus as, 'We must at all costs retain what we have achieved down here'. The new Mark Two Fianna Fáil government quickly saw that, in practical terms, this meant they must sustain the *status quo* in the Six Counties and this became the new national objective. To that end we still deploy with ever-increasing efficiency the full resources of our security forces along the border, imposed by the foreign enemy, where they act on our behalf in concert with Her Majesty's army, Her Majesty's Royal Ulster Constabulary and Her Majesty's Ulster Defence Regiment to defend the integrity of Her Majesty's realm, part of which is defined in the Irish Constitution as part of the national territory which is still pending re-integration!

One result of this is that lawlessness stalks the streets of Dublin with impunity and the cost of the Border joint security is a major factor in our economic ruin. The funny thing about it is that despite the demonstrable fact that the current cost of what is called security is beyond our financial capacity to support the people appear to expect security in the Twenty-six Counties as well! Did anyone ever hear of such arrant nonsense? The Soldiers of Destiny who marched so proudly from the La Scala chanting the Civil War songs like *Take it Down from the Mast, Irish Traitors* and *We'll Crown de Valera King of Ireland,* and who twenty-five years later had marched from the Capitol to the refrain 'Out and make way for the Bold Fenian Men', baulked at the final step which would achieve the national objective but which might eventually lose them the political pre-eminence to which they had become accustomed. From his eyrie above politics in the Phoenix park the retired leader who had given them their original marching orders saw the Mark Time followed by About Turn, Quick March, saw the government performance in the Arms Crisis, saw the growing alignment of the Fianna Fáil government with the British military effort to maintain the integrity of the United Kingdom, remained as President and kept his constitutional silence. He lived to retire again and extended his silence into his retirement. As I skim through the Chief's many speeches on 'the gravest injury one nation can inflict on another', I find myself for some reason thinking of O'Connell's promise to monster meeting after monster meeting that 1843 would be Repeal year, and the aftermath of the turning back at Clontarf.

In the context of the subject of this book, the result of the sudden emergence of the Six County question as the prime political issue in Ireland was the removal of Fianna Fáil from office in circumstances in which a government acting in accordance with the 1926/51 directives or with the unanimous Dáil statement of the national aim, could not conceivably have been defeated. The Fianna Fáil reaction to the refusal of the coerced community in the Six Counties to accept any longer the continuous institutional violence and the periodic physical violence of the Orange mob sponsored by the security forces, precluded the 1973 election being contested on the basis of the most clearly relevant matter. The case for the ending of the Union, based on the fundamental principles of justice, self-determination and democracy, had been officially withdrawn by the Mark Two government. In 1972 I had heard Kennedy, Ribicoff, Carey, Biaggi and many more United States senators and congressmen making the case they had learned well from Mr de Valera over the years before the foreign affairs sub-committee of the Congress and had witnessed the anti-climax when they were debunked by the words of Dr Hillery, then the Minister for External Affairs *(See Appendix B, page 143)*. The party which had set out with such determination in 1926 to remove the 'elected native government under contract with the enemy to maintain his overlordship', and which had responded enthusiastically to the 1951 call to undertake the last remaining step, had accepted the same ignominious contract in much less excusable circumstances. Fianna Fáil could give no special reason for a renewed vote of confidence related to the current repression by British military force of the national aspiration. There was clearly no such reason. There was no Fianna Fáil policy on the matter any more. Instead there was the bi-partisan policy or the unified approach. The bi-partisan policy was not the policy of Fine Gael, which was indelibly on the Dáil record as proposed by Mr John A. Costello, Taoiseach. It was the policy of Cumann na nGaedheal, the one-time government 'under contract with the enemy to maintain his overlordship'. There was no question in 1973 of a rallying slogan such as *Stand by Lynch and Safeguard the Nation,* because Fianna Fáil had unambiguously reneged on the nation as defined in the Constitution, as was recommended by the Colley Committee in 1967 *(see Appendix C, page 145)*. It was acting as the second guarantor of the inviolability of what used to be described as the British-imposed Border; the green-uniformed Óglaigh na hÉireann stood shoulder to shoulder with the storied regiments of Her Majesty's forces in defence of the *status quo;* the Garda Síochana acted as one with the Royal Ulster Constabulary and the revived B Specials, the Ulster Defence Regiment, to preserve the peace of Her Majesty's realm. This would have been unthinkable in 1926 and 1951 and Fianna Fáil were defeated in the 1973 general election. 'Let Erin remember the days of old ere her faithless sons betrayed her.'

They realised from the start that to rely on their erstwhile Republican principles would be seen as both cynical and ridiculous by the voters and, as the campaign progressed, they were clearly losing the argument on economic issues. The result of this and the loss of morale, arising from the shame of their Six County policy, was that they had not the confidence to rely on the established ground of the invariable association of Coalition government with economic crisis and the proven need for financial rectitude. They panicked and, in the later stages of the campaign, they entered into the irresponsible bidding for votes with unjustifiable promises which could not be reconciled with financial probity. Their final bid on rates was identified as a reckless gambler's last despairing plunge and it failed. Nevertheless, it was the commencement of the pattern of irresponsibility on both sides of the political divide which has brought the State to the verge of bankruptcy. If they had the common sense to realise it, this defeat would have been a bit of luck both for the State and for Fianna Fáil. It meant that there was time for the party to pull itself together and to contest the next election on the basis of a simple proposal to once again restore the economy which was obviously going to suffer the same type of recession as under the previous Coalition governments. If they were so inclined, they were also provided with the opportunity to go back to the old, traditional attitude of Fianna Fáil, that the fundamental requirement for peace in Ireland and for goodwill between the people of the two neighbouring islands was the righting of the wrong which Britain continued to perpetrate on the Irish nation. There was, however, a new mentality in the ascendancy based on the influx of new members who believed that everyone had his price. Instead of standing on the policy of financial and fiscal probity which the people are quite capable of understanding if it is put to them by politicians they can trust; instead of forgetting the 1973 aberration which had luckily been rejected in favour of the more attractive wares offered by the Coalition, the people were inflicted with the disaster of the

Think Tank, the faceless backroom strategists thinking only of the purchase of votes with their brainchild — the 1977 Manifesto. The backwoodsmen were allowed the apparent victory of a return on paper to the hallowed traditional policy on the Six Counties question. This was qualified by the leader's announcement that, in practice, the bipartisan policy would continue. The party were told that they could have whatever policy they liked but it would not influence government thinking. They took it lying down.

So history repeated itself. Fianna Fáil had gone out of office for the first time after sixteen years in 1948 three years before the Silver Jubilee and, in 1973, three years before the Golden Jubilee they were out again after another unbroken run of sixteen years. This defeat came four years after the establishment of an apparently invincible position in 1969. It came about solely because of the loss of morale and of the old motivation by the organisation and this, in turn, arose from the knowledge of the members that their basic Republican character was gone. They had, in fact, re-labelled themselves as The Party of Pragmatism some years earlier. Pragmatism may be a good quality but it lacks inspiration because factually it excludes principle. Although the acutal lapsed members were, in the main, readily replaced by a new type of member who came only when the last vestige of the Republican stigma appeared to have gone, it was not possible to produce anything approaching the old-time enthusiasm. I remember Seán Sheridan telling me that when he was director of elections in County Cavan he started off in some fear and trepidation to tell his keymen of the second general election a few months after the election of 1937. The first cumann secretary he approached was hard at work in a meadow literally making hay while the sun shone. 'We're going to have another election,' was Seán's greeting. The reply was, 'Bedammit but it's time', and the hay fork was stuck in the ground while arrangements were made for the convention. That kind of enthusiasm is gone. The fact remains, however, that measured by the pragmatic yardstick of electoral support, the defeat was not by any means a departure from the established pattern. In fact, the Dáil representation was

47.91% and this was the highest figure at which Fianna Fáil
were ever in opposition after an election. It was higher than
the support obtained in 1932 and in 1951. Sixty-nine seats
against seventy-five for all others indicated substantial
majority support, which in normal circumstances would
produce a Fianna Fáil minority government but, for the
first time since 1932, Fianna Fáil's support was not greater
than the total of all the other actual parties. Between them
Fine Gael and Labour had seventy-three seats, so despite
the maintenance of percentage support a proud Fianna Fáil
record was lost. This time there was no reason to expect a
short-lived Coalition government, unless a favourable run
of by-elections changed the Dáil position. This didn't
happen and Fianna Fáil were out of office for their Golden
Jubilee.

I had quite vivid memories of the 1951 commemoration
and, indeed, of the twenty-first anniversary celebrations in
1947. For both of these events special functions were held
throughout the Twenty-six Counties. The main national
event was the special commemoration concert in the
Capitol (La Scala) Theatre and on each occasion the
centrepiece was the first item after the half-time interlude.
This was listed as:

> *Óráid*   Eamon de Valera, TD
> *Cathaoirleach* Pádraig Ruitléis, TD

Needless to say, on each occasion the *Óráid* was a follow-
up to the original 1926 directive. The Silver Jubilee was
marked in a special and permanent way by the publication
of a substantial souvenir brochure outlining the history of
the previous twenty-five years and a copy of this historic
volume still exists in every authentic Fianna Fáil house-
hold. It was a record that enabled every member to see
himself or herself as belonging in the gallant company of
our heroic dead who had striven over the centuries to free
Ireland from the tyrannical grip of the foreign enemy. I had
been looking forward to the inevitable celebrations of 1976
for some time. I thought they would be quite interesting. I
was interested in the prospect of reading the *Óráid* by Jack
Lynch, TD to mark the occasion in the traditional way. It
would, obviously, be somewhat different. To begin with

the national shrine was no more. In the year 1973 when
Fianna Fáil lost office, the Capitol Theatre was demolished. Perhaps this was appropriate because Eamon de
Valera, TD was no longer available and the contrast with
1926, 1947 and 1951 would be too marked.

I was also interested in the history which would be required to complement that published in 1951. I thought this
also would be interesting if it was attempted at all and, although I knew there would be some reluctance, I could not
see how the 1951 precedent could be ignored. Somehow or
other I felt sure that the progress on the line of national advance would not be covered adequately in whatever Jubilee
records were produced. In fact I was so certain of this that I
wrote *Up Dev* primarily to fill the gap that would otherwise
exist in the record of the Achievements which had been
officially listed up to 1951. I would not have been really surprised if the advent of the Jubilee was forgotten altogether
but it wasn't. Fianna Fáil were out of office and the celebration of the fiftieth anniversary could be a useful
springboard for the comeback. In the matter of the history
the decision was to do a really professional job this time.
About two years before the momentous date it was
announced that a prestigious professional historian had
been appointed to edit a full-scale history of the fifty years.
The appointed editor was Mr T. P. O'Neill, of University
College Galway, who had been specially appointed to act
as Mr de Valera's official biographer. He had the advantage of full access to the Chief's papers and long consultation with him on his whole career and, of course, he had
been a witness like everyone else to the events in the party
since Mr de Valera's retirement. There could be no better
qualified man to do the job entrusted to him, but six years
have passed since the Jubilee year and there has been no
explanation, from any source, of the non-appearance of the
promised history. I remember some time after the announcement of his appointment I was a member of a panel
on the television programme *Féach* with Mr O'Neill. The
presenter of the programme, Proinsias Mac Aonghusa,
described him as being the man currently engaged in writing the official history of Fianna Fáil and Mr O'Neill was

very adamant in insisting that he was not writing it. He was to edit the contributions of others and no more. He was emphatic in pointing out that he would have no responsibility for the material in the book. It seemed obvious to me that even at that early stage there were problems arising for his professional integrity as a historian. That was to be expected. The objective truth could only be damaging to the party. Whatever the problems were the history announced with a fanfare of trumpets never saw the light of day, although it is widely believed that the material for it was compiled. Its non-appearance was surely a matter calling for some consideration by any political correspondent worthy of his calling but there was a unanimous decision to spare Fianna Fáil this embarrassment. Not alone was there no speculation as to the reason for this debacle there was no mention of it at all. This was, of course, a continuation of the blanket cover-up by all sections of the media of the most disgraceful incident in the public life of this country — the scandalous performance of the Fianna Fáil government in the matter of the Arms Crisis or Non-crisis and the endorsement of these standards by the Dáil and the Fianna Fáil organisation at all levels. What was it, exactly, that the powers that be wanted to have included in the history, with which the distinguished editor, de Valera's biographer, could not agree, even though his function as editor did not require his endorsement of the views expressed? Or was it that something was to be excluded, which could not be excluded from a book edited by a reputable historian and claiming to be a history? Or was it that the editor insisted that he, as editor, had both the right and the duty to disclaim any responsibility for the versions of particular matters given in the body of the book which were clearly contrary to fact? No one knows the answer to these questions because none of our fearless investigative journalists investigated the matter. This was a matter of legitimate interest to the members of the public interested in political matters and particularly to those anxious to bring their official history of Fianna Fáil up to date. These latter can, of course, fill the gap on their bookshelves with *Up Dev*. The only reasonable explanation I can see is that there was a rigid decision by media controllers that the unsavoury matter safely and efficiently swept under the carpet by them in 1970 was to stay there undisturbed. This decision was endorsed by the Coalition parties and, needless to say enthusiastically agreed to by both wings of Fianna Fáil. The party which so proudly chronicled, in permanent form, the events of its first twenty-five years, was ashamed to do the same for its most recent history. The loyal Fianna Fáil households, which are the proud owners of the story of the first twenty-five years, have no corresponding record of the second twenty-five years. No wonder the children are not so consistently following in their fathers' footsteps.

In 1951, deputies and ministers went all over the Twenty-six Counties talking to the organisation of their reason for joining the new movement twenty-five years earlier, of their pride in the record of achievement and of their view of the party now and of its future. In 1976, the successors hung their heads in shame, as though to say 'Let us not dwell on the past' but 'lift up your eyes unto the deathless morrow, and greet the light that surely must break there.' The thing to do was to get the embarrassing matter of the Jubilee celebrations out of the way as quickly and unobtrusively as possible. So, instead of the promised history with its status as such authenticated, however obliquely, by the editing of a professional historian who was an authority on the subject, we had merely a peculiar twelve page supplement issued with *The Irish Press* on the 26 May 1976. Instead of the publicly announced editing of the history, we had a half page article in the supplement written by Mr T. P. O'Neill, headed 'Birth of the Party' which turned out to be a potted history. Potted, as it was, Mr O'Neill being a historian could not omit the skeleton in the cupboard and this is how he dealt with it:

The troubles in the north-east of this island had repercussions south of the border. There was considerable heart-searching. The leader of Fianna Fáil, Jack Lynch, who had succeeded Seán Lemass in 1966, won a great electoral victory in 1969.

Lynch became the only Irish leader, apart from de Valera, to lead a party to an overall majority since the foundation of the State. The disturbances and the heart-search-

ing raised difficulties for his government. It led to differences in the Cabinet and consequent resignations and
demotions.

A nice innocuous way to describe these events, but then it
is not a historian's function to do a white-wash job, and Mr
O'Neill, who is one of the most competent and highly regarded historians, did not in fact do so. What he wrote was
simply an understatement and after all this was only a con-
densed history. So, with no more than a grin, one can let
terminology like considerable heart-searching, difficulties
for his government and demotions pass as references to
things which were regarded as bomb shells at the time. This
time there was no commemorative concert, no *Óráid* by
the leader to inspire the Soldiers of Destiny to even greater
effort in the years to come. As I have said, Fianna Fáil's
national shrine had fallen to the rapacious developer and,
with the traditional platform gone, Mr Lynch decided not
to match words with his illustrious predecessor. Where
would he get a suitable platform? The Theatre Royal was
also gone. The substitute for the *Óráid* was an introduction
to the supplement by the leader. This was an almost ran-
dom collection of banal, virtually meaningless clichés. At
least it was appropriate. There was also a pictorial record,
which included photographs of all Fianna Fáil governments
but one — an extra punishment for the miscreants who had
failed to follow where the one true leader led. For them, in
addition to excommunication, there was the ignominy of
not being in the pictorial record.

So, the faithful had the supplement and a pictorial record
published by *The Irish Press*, which would not survive the
years. With the great occasion thus adequately marked,
what would they want with a formal written history edited
by a pernickety historian? Fianna Fáil was never a party to
paint the lily! This incident pinpoints two aspects of the real
decline of Fianna Fáil, election results notwithstanding.
They are ashamed of themselves from the Republican and
public morality points of view. The September 1982 edition
of *Magill*, which tells us that the now loyal, and erstwhile
dissident, wing of Fianna Fáil, in cataloguing yet another
notable Jubilee, the twenty-five years Dáil career of

Charles Haughey, found it necessary to omit the six year period from the dismissal to the second coming. A common sense of shame is, apparently, the only uniting bond between the various factions. Maybe it is better than nothing. There is some hope for the miscreant who can still feel ashamed. Perhaps this applies to political parties as well.

8

The Third Twenty-Five Years

The third twenty-five year period of Fianna Fáil history began in May 1976 with the Coalition in office for just over three years. They had to wait another year for a general election. When it came they maintained their record of never losing two elections in succession. In 1981 they were out again but in the next year, nine years after the end of their second sixteen year period of office, they were back again, thus repeating the pattern of 1948-57. Now all they have to do to maintain the established rhythm is to stay in office for another sixteen years. A lot of knowledgeable people have their doubts about their ability to do this. Whatever happens one thing is certain, the most recent figures of electoral support give no indication of the coming collapse which is being so widely forecast. The figures for Dáil support were 56.76% in 1977, 46.99% in 1981 and 48.79% in 1982. The latter figure is very near the average for all elections since and including 1932 and, of course, if Neil Blaney is taken into account as he normally is by the experts in similar computations, it approaches even closer to the average and also to 50%.

The 1977 result is particularly interesting and the way it was obtained is even more so, marking as it does a very significant turning point and indicating the change in character of Fianna Fáil. The 56.76% support achieved in 1977 is the greatest ever obtained by any party since the foundation of the Irish Free State, being almost 1% higher than in 1938. This was a majority of twenty seats in a Dáil of one hundred and forty-eight, while in 1938 the majority was sixteen seats in a Dáil of one hundred and thirty-eight. The fact that, in 1938, the percentage first preference vote was greater than in 1977 by 1.3% may indicate that the spectacular national achievements of the earlier period were less attractive to Fianna Fáil's opponents than the promised goodies of 1977. On the other hand, the substantially higher differential between actual support and first preference votes may be merely a reflection of the fact that the revision of constituencies carried out by the Coalition government was patently devised so as to produce a decisive result one way or the other. As always after a period of the Coalition, the climate was favourable for a change and the result was decisive. Some might say that the margin of victory was excessive but the thing that made the 1977 victory so significant and of such major importance was not the magnitude of the majority but the manner in which it was obtained. In the circumstances there could be no question of possible failure to achieve a return to office unless the whole party structure collapsed and, bad as morale was, there was no danger of that. It is true that the organisation was not the organisation of old although it was numerically as strong as ever and it had previously undreamed of funds at its disposal. The party that contested the previous election in 1973 was unlike Fianna Fáil at any other stage in its history. The shadow of the Arms Trial loomed large. There was, for instance, Mr Lynch, the accuser as Taoiseach, Mr Gibbons, the chief witness for the prosecution as Minister for Agriculture and Mr Haughey, the accused as Honorary Secretary, belying the façade of unity. Each side had and was known to have their supporters. There was internal intrigue, the appearance of unity was no more than a veneer, and the party was beginning to lack credibility. For the first time in a general election there was speculation as to whether all the key figures wanted a victory. In 1977, after four years in opposition — longer opposition than the party had experienced since 1932 — the intrigue was more widespread and less discreet. During the period out of office, in a despairing effort to regain the lost Republican motivation, a new statement of policy on the Six Counties more in line with the traditional attitude had been forced through against the determined and open opposition of the leadership. This was a measure of the extent and success of the dissidence in the party and it was publicly displayed. Nevertheless, the old taboo of the inviolability of the titular leader, wherever or however he might lead, stood the test and as long as the semblance of unity remained the circumstances were such as to ensure a Fianna Fáil victory.

The Coalition had done it again. The economy was in ruins. There were, of course, adverse international circumstances and there was the EEC super-government to which the people themselves had ceded the power to control economic trends but this did not matter: it was the third time out of three chances. To a Fianna Fáil organisation in the whole of its health no more than this circumstance was needed to win the election and in 1977 there were other favourable circumstances in abundance — but Fianna Fáil had changed, its fighting spirit was gone. The loss of morale, of cohesion, of idealistic motivation and of pride, was such that they lacked the self-confidence to ask the people to let them undertake the urgently necessary restoration job yet again and to more or less leave it at that. They had not got that degree of confidence in one another and, naturally, they did not expect the electorate to trust them implicitly either. There were other factors in their favour as well as the disastrous state of the economy. The people, for instance, had seen the type of regime already emerging which could be expected to develop further from the continuance of a Fine Gael dominated government. They had also seen the clear signs of the jackboot mentality particularly in the attitude of the Taoiseach, Mr Cosgrave, the Minister for Justice, Mr Cooney and the Minister for Defence, Mr Donegan, but as if that was not enough, they saw on television the blood-chilling spectre of unrepentant Blueshirtism at the Fine Gael Ard Fheis. From this it was clear that the draconian attitude of the leadership was no more than a reflection of the ordinary membership and they were frightened at what this presaged. The tragedy for the State was that because of the fundamental change in the nature of the Fianna Fáil party, the so-obviously favourable circumstances were not recognised as sufficient. I still find it difficult to credit this but, apparently, they actually believed or had become brainwashed by the propaganda invented by some academic expert who was never involved in an election in his life into believing that the Coalition revision of the constituencies was a fiendishly clever plan to prevent the people from carrying out their democratic function of returning Fianna Fáil to power. In any case they had the wherewithal to replace the damaged morale of the organisation and had laid their plans to use it. Arising out of Coalition fiscal legislation they had finance from big business sources on a virtually unlimited scale. As a result they now had provided themselves with back-up services and a think-tank of experts. The Cumainn and Comhairlí Ceanntair, which had sufficed as the eyes and ears of the organisation for so long, were superseded and downgraded to the status of mere unskilled labourers in the political vineyard. The think-tank had been given the task of winning the election. They set about doing this with gusto and produced a set of election-winning proposals. There was no denying that. The snag was that they were beyond the capacity of the economy in its existing state of organisation to provide. Because the appointed strategists were entirely ignorant of practical politics no one could see that in the factual situation the revision of the constituencies itself ensured their return, and no one could see that, think-tank or no think-tank, the wise thing to do was to say no more than was required and so they had to have all this and the Manifesto too. That was the rock we all perished on.

It was an entirely new situation in Irish politics. The postwar established pattern was a period of Coalition recklessness and instability followed by a Fianna Fáil repair job and then economic expansion. After the first Coalition period of government there was an attempted Fianna Fáil restoration from 1951 to 1954. The second Coalition produced the full-scale disaster of 1957. For the next sixteen years, whatever other criticisms there might be, we had financial rectitude and economic stability which started to deteriorate only when the Fianna Fáil party lost its integrity and its nerve. Now we had for the first time ever two successive general elections on the basis of each side trying to outbid the other for the irresponsible type of support. It was a formula for certain economic disaster. In the 1977 election there was no way the public could make a decision to avoid the catastrophic situation which has resulted. Whatever way it turned out we were to have for the first time a second successive period of gross irresponsibility. That was what the welter of promises amounted to. Obviously it would be much more difficult, in any circumstances, to recover from two such periods than from one but now any elected government's hands were tied. The necessary measures to save our economy would be in breach of the EEC laws framed, as they are, specifically and totally for the well-being of the unscrupulous, capitalist profiteers of Europe. So a government endeavouring to correct the disaster of the Fianna Fáil Manifesto following on the disaster of the 1973 Coalition must stand futilely by and watch our industries closing down at the dictates of the pragmatic European bureaucracy, and watch our farmers and horticulturalists destroying their produce for a mere token monetary compensation. It is illegal to have the only realistic type of *Buy Irish* campaign possible, that is, to base it solidly on the prevention of dumping by the European financial interests who find our market essential to their viability in present circumstances. So what can we do? Appeal to the patriotism of the supermart owners? We want our collective head examined. From the day when, under the guidance of Fianna Fáil, the people were conned into ceding control of our economy to the ultra-selfish big business alignment of our European partners, anything in the nature of a *Buy Irish* campaign became a cruel cynical joke and an unjustifiable waste of money and effort. Small wonder that earlier this season (1982) there were signs of reversion to traditional forms of agrarian violence to counter the dumping of foreign produce on the Irish market.

The tragedy about this is that it was so completely unnecessary. Fianna Fáil before its metamorphosis when the members still had their national aim to sustain their fortitude and when those who were involved in party strategy and tactics had not to keep an alert eye to their rear would have understood this and there would have been no think-tank and no Manifesto, but then, come to think of it, if the change in the party had not come about they would not have been out of office. It would not, of course, be fair to say the think-tank was a failure. It had done the job allotted to it with the professional efficiency to which its members laid claim. It had produced the greatest majority of all time and there was nothing in its brief about ensuring the stability of the economy. They had been told to produce a set of proposals the voters would buy and the voters had certainly bought the Manifesto. It had therefore proved its superiority to the old, antedeluvian process of policy developing unscientifically but democratically by mysterious means from impulses initiated at Cumann level. There is a fallacy in that reasoning. The think-tank, after the manner of academics dealing in the abstract, had shown its capacity to produce the package it was programmed to produced, but the Cumann members knew the reality of financial constraints. In their private and political lives they knew there were desirable things which were not immediately obtainable. The old system might have produced a smaller majority. So what?

Each of the two periods of irresponsible government lasted for four years, so we had eight successive years of it. It is true that midway through the second period there was a change to a new leader who was reputed to be opposed to the Manifesto. This occurred when, in reaction to the fear of losing their seats induced by the results of actually attempting to implement in the real world the ridiculous, wishful-thinking of the Manifesto, the Fianna Fáil backbenchers ousted Mr Lynch as Taoiseach. The unthinkable had happened; the leader had been downed, caught by the pack and savaged; but the new incumbent, Mr Haughey, had existed on a diet of humble pie for so long that he became addicted to it. He had not the nerve to tackle the job, to confront his Cabinet colleagues and openly abandon the lunacy of the Manifesto, and a reasonable chance to rescue the economy was lost. He had not the nerve to confront them on the national issue either, as many people expected him to do, even with a formally adopted party policy document of recent date in existence not merely authorising but requiring a change. Instead of a change back to the traditional attitude, participation in the British military effort was intensified. The roll of Irish martyrs was augmented by Mrs Thatcher's contribution of

MAY THE BRITS PAY FOR THE BORDER SECURITY Bill

ten dead hunger-strikers, while the Fianna Fáil government stood idly by, and in 1981 in a Dáil increased to one hundred and sixty-six seats, Fianna Fáil won six less than they gained in 1977, when the total of seats was one hundred and forty-eight. As far as the economy at least was concerned the 1977 election was the most significant and most disastrous since the founding of the State. Despite the twenty seat majority, it may yet prove to have been equally disastrous for Fianna Fáil. One ray of hope is that rumour has it that the finances which made the think-tank possible are to be withdrawn.

Fianna Fáil's 1981 nosedive in Dáil representation at 9.77%, from 56.76% to 46.99%, broke the previous record for the drop in support from one election to another but it was only marginally greater than in 1948 when it fell by 8.81% from 55.07% to 46.26% and since it fell from a higher figure the resulting position was in fact slightly better than in 1948. After eight years of irresponsibility, things were so bad that the incoming Coalition had no option but to try to assume the mantle of financial rectitude which they were not structured to carry particularly since this time their existence as government was in the hands of a small group of left-wing deputies, the inevitable product of economic crisis. They did make an effort, albeit an inadequate one, but with typical lack of acumen they miscalculated how far their controllers on the left would allow them to go. In the resulting general election of 1982 Fianna Fáil although, as already mentioned, getting almost half the seats (counting Neil Blaney), just failed to make the required number. They are back in government at the whim of people whose dearest wish is to destroy them, their leader in particular, and the democratic system as we know it. They have lost one by-election, which they created themselves, in a constituency in which there was no reason based on publicly known fact why they should hope much less expect to win and they have won the other by-election in a constituency in which it was almost impossible for them to lose. There has been no untoward loss of support in either case. So there is still no factual sign of deterioration electorally. Throughout all the demonstrable degeneration of the party intrinsically, they have consistently managed and are still managing to hold their own where it counts as far as a pragmatic political party is concerned — in the ballot boxes. Why, then, does almost everyone say they are on the way out?

9

Real Decline

Judging by media comment and from listening to people who claim to have supported Fianna Fáil in the recent past there appears to be a fairly widespread feeling that the party has been and possibly still is declining. Many predict a substantial collapse at the polls next time out. I have pointed out that there are absolutely no figures to substantiate this but it does not necessarily follow that either the belief or the forecast is wrong. The question to be answered is: whether a pragmatic political party can factually decline while still prospering electorally? I start with the presumption that a decline in real terms may not necessarily be accompanied immediately by electoral collapse although one must expect the democratic process to catch up and eventually reflect the situation. I maintain that, nothwithstanding the maintenance of electoral support, Fianna Fáil has declined in every other way. The great difficulty for the average voter is to find what he or she will regard as a real alternative. If he insists that the alternative must be a readymade alternative instant majority party catering for the Republican outlook, he is asking too much unless Fianna Fáil were to go into voluntary liquidation. For the type of voter who has consistently supported Fianna Fáil, there is no such alternative. Fine Gael and Labour are unthinkable, particularly from the national point of view. The result is that disillusioned supporters see no alternative but to hope for a miracle to restore Fianna Fáil to what it was. For the not-so-thoroughly-committed voter the recent proof that the Blueshirt mentality is very much alive and well must remain a very strong factor inducing a sense of futility about the present state of affairs. It is the public demonstration, in the wake of the 1982 election, of the appallingly low calibre of the present parliamentary party that has created the belief that the decline in figures cannot be far away. How can decent people be expected to vote for them?

There surely cannot be any doubt that the public exhibition so many members of the parliamentary party made of themselves prior to the election of Taoiseach, marks a very real and substantial decline in the quality of the party in what is regarded as the top echelon. This was not confined to those believed to be in contention for the leadership; backbenchers contributed equally to the overall picture of a party composed of real-life caricatures of the politician motivated only by self interest. The general public reaction was one of shock at finding that the largest political party, which had obviously been given a reasonably clear mandate to form the government, was apparently in an advanced stage of decomposition. There was no cohesion, no united front, no sense of determination to tackle the stupendous problems resulting from at least nine years of culpable mismanagement; there was a complete absence of team-spirit and, therefore, no reason to expect success. Instead, there was an unsavoury parade of people interested only in advancing themselves at the expense of their colleagues, displaying no concern for the gigantic task facing them as a government party but all engaged in a game of unscrupulous intrigue in which virtually no one was to be trusted. It was the most disedifying political spectacle ever seen here with the single exception of the series of events lumped together under the title 'The Arms Crisis'. It was not merely disedifying; it was frightening because it was difficult to expect the problems afflicting the State to be solved by any government formed from a selection of the people involved. There was, however, no justification for shock because this was all clearly the result of the low standards of personal behaviour openly adopted by the government and party in 1970 and it was within the knowledge of every voter that this was so. There must have been people who could see the contrast with the earlier Fianna Fáil governments from 1932 to 1948, which methodically and with determination dismantled the Irish Free State and developed the economy to the stage where it was possible to remain neutral in the Second World War, and with the government which in 1957 undertook the restoration and further development of the wrecked economy, which kept its unity of purpose through two changes of leadership and maintained the economy in a sound condition in a changing world — until 1969-70, when it disintegrated in the reneging of its basic national aim. There was for all to see an unmistakable and catastrophic decline in the party, whatever the election figures said. It was rotten, and compared unfavourably with every other government since 1922, whether Cumann na nGaedheal, Fianna Fáil or Coalition. It is no wonder if people are asking themselves if a government composed of these elements could do the job required? The obvious deterioration in the quality of the personnel at parliamentary party level, although it is probably the basic cause, is only one aspect of the decline.

Considering first only pragmatic political qualities, there is a deterioration in the quality of political judgement in matters of both tactics and broad strategy, and in the courage to adhere without deviation to decisions taken in the conviction that they are necessary. I have already referred to instances of this and there is no need to go into these any further. The instances of poor judgement since the 1982 general election, however, are currently relevant. One such example is the bidding for independent support after the election which was entirely inexcusable from the point of view of public decency and respect for democracy. It was also thoroughly bad tactics. The Fianna Fáil party of which I was a member would have left the bargaining to the experts in bargaining, the two parties which had sustained themselves for thirty-four years since 1948 by a continuing process of bargaining with one another and with whatever other groups or individuals were available at any given time. With Fianna Fáil's thirty-four years experience as observers of the results of the bargaining process which always worked out ultimately to their advantage, the party should have seen that this time the Coalition would certainly be hoist their own petard. They should have stood aloof with their eighty-one seats and let the Fine Gael leader do the bidding if he was so inclined. If the left-wing group were to consider their own long-term prospects, they would have to get a deal which the Fine Gael leader could not give, if he was to retain any credibility with his own supporters. The group to be conciliated included some of those who had put the Coalition government out, and if they were to be accommodated the issue on which the election was fought would have to be conceded. Mr Haughey should have let them at it and if they so decided put back the government they had ejected, this time with a more securely tied millstone round its neck. If he had the nerve to do this, the ultimate result would be a swing to Fianna Fáil, which would enable a proper policy to be pursued as well as establishing his leadership on a sound basis. There was also the possibility that the Coalition might not succeed in getting the necessary support and that Fianna Fáil would be allowed to form a minority government. This would have been better than the resulting situation. It might have been a government without any committed outside support but it would be a government without strings attached. As it was it is clear that whether the outside support was committed or not it was, in fact, forthcoming only as long as it suited. Such a Fianna Fáil government, if it retained the old backbone, would have acted as the situation required irrespective of its position in the Dáil. This might have meant another election, a return to the pattern of 1933, 1938 and 1944, and a Fianna Fáil organisation retaining its old morale would react as before, 'Bedammit, but it's time for another election to settle this matter'. But, of course, things were not as they had been; the leader was no longer inviolate; the knives were not being sharpened; they had already been honed in public and were poised for the leader's back. Whether it was an uncontrollable lust for power or fear of the enemies within the gates the decision was to buy support at a price that would militate severely against any effort to restore the damaged economy — and it wasn't even a gentleman's agreement between people whose word was their bond nor even a document setting out the deal and signed by the dealers. The level of mutual trust was so high that a non-elected, total outsider had to be brought in to append his signature as a witness — yet another unworthy precedent which demeans our demo-

cracy. It did at least enable the leader to keep ahead of the
ravening pack for a little while.

This characteristic which is new to Fianna Fáil, being
manifested publicly for the first time in the 1973 general
election, is an indirect by-product of the loss of self-confidence and self-esteem and this, in turn, arises from the
reneging of the basic national principle, the full alignment
with the British military effort in the Six Counties and the
formal discarding of the high moral principles on which the
original leadership placed such importance. Once the party
adopted the role of second guarantor for the permanence
of Partition, the members at all levels knew it was no longer
the national movement. The line of national advance had
been abandoned and there was nothing left but self-
interest. The only motivation was to preserve the party for
its own sake. There was no longer any principle involved.
Deprived as they were of self-esteem and their sense of
national purpose which sustained them for so long in every
trial and tribulation, judgement and tactics became a
matter of assessing what was the short-term politically
expedient course to take on every issue without any underlying guiding principle. It was a question of deciding what
course of action or what set of proposals were best calcu-
lated to secure support from whatever quarter it appeared
to be obtainable. In some instances it was a case of —
'There goes the mob. I must follow. I am its leader.' In
others it was as the old proverb inelegantly puts it, a case of
lying down with dogs and getting up with fleas. Of course,
particularly since the institution of the Fianna Fáil version
of Lynching, faulty decisions may also be partly due to the
fact that full and frank consultation with the members of
the government or front bench is no longer feasible. Collective responsibility is a joke because there is no longer a
common interest to be served. The group with whom the
leader might expect, and be expected, to consult on important matters requiring a personal initiative by him
obviously includes people whose interests would be best
served by a wrong decision. It is, then, my contention that
the frequently inept vacillating and sometimes palpably
scandalous performance of the Fianna Fáil party derives

from the fundamental change in the character of the party, which has taken place over a period of years. In an article in the April 1982 *Magill* magazine, I have already stated my opinion that Fianna Fáil has changed in three ways:—

I

Fianna Fáil was formed almost exclusively from the Republicans defeated in the Civil War. It consisted, then, originally of people who had dedicated themselves at an early age to the breaking of the connection with England and the establishment of the Irish Republic, who had endured the rigours of guerrilla war, who refused to take the easy and lucrative way with the Treaty and, therefore, endured the Civil War, further imprisonment and in many cases a long hunger-strike. They were all people who had already sacrificed some of the most valuable years of their lives in the national cause who could say like Pearse's 'Fool': 'I have squandered the splendid years, that the Lord God gave to my youth, in attempting impossible things, deeming them alone worth the toil.' The party they joined was dedicated to the achievement of the same ideal, so it was reasonable to expect discipline and integrity from them. Nevertheless, this was a political party which would be contesting elections to an established parliament, even though it was one whose legitimacy was not accepted by the new party, and it was realised that not everyone who is attracted to politics is actuated by the purest of motives. From the very outset there was a fully promulgated, though unwritten, rule that any departure from a high standard of personal integrity would entail expulsion from the party. During the time of Mr de Valera's leadership there were a number of cases in which this rule was implemented at different levels of the party. Some of these were publicly known, while others would have been known only locally. I am not aware of any case of expulsion for this reason since Mr de Valera's retirement although I am satisfied that some cases that would have been dealt with in this way under the earlier regime, did arise. The accepted principle now seems to be that a

'person's private life is his own business'. It sounds reasonable enough until it is examined and it seems to be accepted
by the Irish public. To the best of my knowledge it is not
accepted in any other genuine democracy. It is a principle
that is not appropriate to a person who opts for public life
and it is one that is dangerous from the point of view of
public morality and the proper conduct of the State's
affairs.

This new attitude was part of a general trend which pre-
disposed the party to adopt the standards formally endorsed in the Motion of Confidence passed by the Dáil on 4
November 1970. Another aspect was the changed
approach to the responsibility of membership of the
government by some ministers appointed since the retirement of Mr de Valera. It was no longer the case of a group
of 'comrades in arms' pursuing a common objective in a
totally unified and selfless way. For the first time de-
partmental policies became identified with the minister
concerned rather than with Fianna Fáil. Mr Seán Lemass
had, of course, always been specifically identified with industrial development, but his reputation was as a very successful promoter of Fianna Fáil policy. Every disagreement
was sorted out at the government table and every detail of
policy was the policy of the Fianna Fáil government once it
had been decided. There were a few cases of ministers not
adequately defending certain aspects of policy, when under
severe pressure, but these were always cleared up and were
generally accepted as instances of momentary weakness
rather than a breach of collective responsibility.

After the retirement of the founding leader, however,
the new phenomenon of Fianna Fáil ministers positively
engaged in promoting their own image at the expense of
their colleagues emerged. This may have been partly due to
the fact that government meetings became less frequent,
shorter and more businesslike but with less than comprehensive examination of proposals. Ministers were encouraged to solve problems of detail themselves rather
than to bring them to the government so that their colleagues in other departments could give their opinions.
There may, or may not, have been greater efficiency but

there certainly was a weakening of the spirit of collective responsibility. The party as a whole began to see real or imagined rivalries and jealousies and the general sense of solidarity was weakened. Jealously and rivalry became an accepted fact of life in the constituencies and the organisation, which had always refused to tolerate this attitude in their representatives, gradually began to take sides. It was another aspect of the slide which accelerated after 1970 until in 1982 the party plumbed the depths of disunity, publicly displaying more intense animosities than had ever been associated with the various Coalitions. This new characteristic of disunity surely reached its apex or its nadir in the 1982 general election when personal rumours of a scandalous nature which have followed Mr Haughey for all his political career were whispered at the voter's doors by Fianna Fáil canvassers. I heard most of these, in one form or another, when he first aspired to contest an election for Dublin Corporation a long time ago, but this is the first time they were really efficiently used. As far as I can gather, in most if not all constituencies, there was a group of canvassers assuring voters in regard to these rumours that they could safely vote for a designated candidate or candidates because, 'After the election we'll have a new leader'. It certainly happened in my area. What an argument! 'We are contesting this election under Mr Haughey as leader, but the first thing we're going to do after the election is depose him.' This is one promise they tried to honour after the election. How could anyone vote for a candidate being promoted in this way? It was a sign of a shifty character unsuited to be a public representative. In these circumstances, eighty-one seats for Fianna Fáil out of one hundred and sixty-six certainly shows a tremendous determination not to have a Coalition at any cost and the public display of the calibre of the party, after the election, was an indication of the high cost paid.

I have dealt at some length in *Up Dev* with the Motion of Confidence passed on 4 November 1970, its meaning and the events leading up to it. The motion was to express confidence in the Taoiseach and the members of the government and it was in the context of the performance in the

high court. It is a matter of publicly established and universally known fact that such confidence was not justified.
Wherever one reads about the Arms Crisis, and there is
quite a bibliography on this subject by now, there is only
one possible conclusion. The only course which could even
partially have saved the honour of the government was
spontaneous resignation and failing resignation the public
interest required their rejection by the Dáil, while the
integrity of the Fianna Fáil organisation required similar
action. In fact, it is not necessary to read any assessment of
the affair at all. All that is required is to read the factual
day-by-day, almost verbatim reports of the completed and
the abortive trials in any of the daily newspapers and the
relevant Dáil reports. Now that there has been a new and
spectacular manifestation of what Fianna Fáil has become
this affair, which is the source of the deterioration of standards, is of renewed public importance. I re-iterate my
challenge to any of the national dailies to publish, even in a
limited edition, a booklet of its own day-by-day reports of
the trials without any comment whatever. Newspapers do
not survive and this is something that should be on permanent record for posterity, if the present generation is not
interested.

Just as there is no need at this stage to establish the facts
since they are known, so also there is no need to elaborate
on the significance for the morality of the whole Fianna Fáil
party as such, of the Arms Trial, the 1970 Motion of Confidence and the endorsement of the 1971 Ard Fheis. Since
1970 every member of the party at every level from front
bench or government to cumann has been living in the full
knowledge of the new standards of public morality
adopted, with the greatest formality, by the party. This was
bound to have its effect on them. Surely they can see now
that the squalid spectacle they have made of themselves
was the inevitable result of deciding to endorse the disgraceful decision of the parliamentary party in 1970? This is
the aspect of decline which is totally beyond dispute. It is
known to every individual in the State and it is and has been
tolerated. Why, then, should there now be surprise or
shock at the quality of the Fianna Fáil parliamentary party?

II

I have mentioned the decision to accept the first big subscription. This had no immediate apparent effect on the character of the party. It was not long, however, until it started to affect the finances. Other subscriptions of the order of a whole constituency's national collection followed the first. Not many, it must be said, but enough to make the financial position more comfortable. It was still true that the wealthy classes were almost exclusively Fine Gael supporters. As the Fianna Fáil industrial policy progressed, however, the ranks of the upper classes were infiltrated by newcomers who had not inherited their wealth but who were becoming modestly wealthy through their own enterprise and industry and through government policy. Not surprisingly some of these became subscribers either on an annual basis or at election time or both. There was still no question of Fianna Fáil getting anything approaching the amount of this type of finance that was always available to Fine Gael. The only noticeable effect on the organisation was that there were complaints from constituencies in which the national collection was carried out from door to door, that people were telling them they always sent their subscription direct to headquarters. Eventually an election finance committee was formed. This was an adhoc group of businessmen who came together at election time and collected subscriptions from their colleagues in the business world and it was formed on their own initiative. The party strategy was that this money collected at one election would be kept in reserve for the next election. The organisation would still have to raise finance locally to the best of their ability but, again, the local fundraising efforts were affected by the potential big subscribers who claimed they always sent their subscriptions direct to headquarters. It became quite a bone of contention.

There was still no obvious change in the character of the organisation although it was a far cry from a few years earlier when it was deemed un-Republican to accept such subscriptions at all. All the time, however, the government was becoming more involved with the entrepreneurial class. This was inevitable given the policy of economic development but not everybody realised the importance of always being on guard against confusing the means with the end. Although its policies were increasing employment opportunities and national output and improving workers' living standards, Fianna Fáil was not the small man's party in the same sense as it was originally. The small man's welfare was becoming the incidental by-product of economic development rather than development being for the purpose of utilising the resources of the State for the benefit of the people as a whole. Generally speaking it was only at or near the top level this subtle change took place. The actual organisation was not affected and did not notice any change in emphasis.

It was shortly after I first became a member of the national executive that I saw the first obvious danger sign. This was the proposal to establish a new extra-mural group to be called Comh-Comhairle Átha Cliath. There were just a few who considered the idea objectionable as soon as it was proposed, but it was presented as a means of financing a new re-organisation drive which was seen as necessary to dispose of the new Coalition menace and this argument carried the day. It was a most peculiar scheme viewed in the context of the constitution and rules of the party. Each constituency organisation in the Dublin area would nominate five members at its annual general meeting to form the nucleus of the group. This was an obvious afterthought from which the title Comh-Comhairle was derived. The general membership would consist of people who for one reason or another had not come to the point of being prepared to join Fianna Fáil or who for obvious reasons could not be expected to be actual members of a political party and who would pay an annual subscription of £10, an undreamt of amount in those days. Apart from financing the re-organisation drive they would constitute an audience who could be invited to hear ministers or front benchers making important statements and they could also provide a forum for discussion based on talks or lectures given by experts in different fields of activity.

There were objections.

'This was to be a Top Hat organisation, beyond the financial scope of the ordinary Fianna Fáil members, to be cossetted by the top brass. The real organisation was to be downgraded and by-passed in the matter of these important statements.'

'No. The new body in actual fact would not be part of the organisation at all. It would have no function in the party but the party would benefit from the subscriptions.'

'Would the members be members of Fianna Fáil?'

'Not necessarily. Membership would continue to be through the cumainn only and unless a member of Comh-Comhairle was already a member of a cumann, he could become a member of the party only by joining a cumann in the normal way. Some might be thinking of joining and no doubt their membership of Comh-Comhairle would help them to make the right decision. The organisation as a whole in the Dublin area would benefit from the fact that five delegates from each constituency would be attending the meetings and functions.'

'Some might not be supporters at all?'

'This was possible but these would be indoctrinated and they would have no influence on policy, which would be a matter for the Ard Fheis, at which they would have no representation. The constituency representatives would have a watching brief for the organisation.'

The objections were overcome.

This peculiar body was established and the re-organisation drive was deemed to be a success. Five members from each Dublin constituency got the opportunity of rubbing shoulders with their betters and of exchanging views with them, workers hobnobbing with bosses and the Top Hat element paid the astronomical fee of £10 per annum, while the constituency representatives were members of the club for free! I think the first meeting of Comh-Comhairle heard Mr Lemass's important statement about a way in which the economy could establish 100,000 new jobs, if the section of the community with the money to invest made certain decisions. I never knew much about the membership because I never liked the idea, but I know some of them who either were indoctrinated and joined or were thinking of joining and made the right decision. I think it would have been better if they had remained in external association or, better still, joined Fine Gael.

The next development of this kind was more sophisticated, in keeping with the increasing sophistication of the new recruits to the party. It was not secret but there was no organised publicity as in the case of Comh-Comhairle Átha Cliath. This did not prevent it being a much more spectacular development. After the second referendum on the proposal to change the voting system, Fianna Fáil were no longer in the position of having the national election collection as a nest-egg for the next election. It was suggested at a meeting of the national executive that the possibility of giving the election finance committee some formal standing and keeping it in being on a permanent basis should be examined. The recommendation of the sub-committee appointed for this purpose was that a total of five hundred people should be invited to join a new group whose function would be to provide election finance for the party. The members would pay an annual subscription of £100 each; the name suggested was Taca, meaning 'support', and the provision of financial support would be the only function of the group. There was less discussion about this. Everyone knew of the election finance committee and the important part it played in augmenting the sinews of war in the time of need, and this was merely a re-vamping of it. The recommendation was accepted and Taca was formed. The idea was that the five hundred subscriptions would be collected and lodged in a special Taca account. There it would remain for a year. The group would finance its activites (a small number of functions were visualised) with the interest for one year on the £50,000 and at the end of the year the £50,000 would be lodged in a Fianna Fáil election account. This procedure would continue from year to year. The businessman mentality was very evident in the scheme. The election account would be under the control of three people, the Taoiseach, one of the joint honorary treasurers and one of the joint honorary secretaries. Money could be withdrawn only over the signatures of two of the three trustees. There was, however, a mistake. The three people were specified by name as Mr J. Lynch, Mr N. Blaney and myself and thereby hangs a tale. It was a little light relief to me when I was already some years in what is described as the wilderness, to be approached by one of the biggest of big businessmen, in what he no doubt regarded as a very skilful and diplomatic manner to liberate a sum of £60,018.65 for the purpose for which it was subscribed in the distant past when there was one fold and one shepherd. I didn't know him but as he went through his act I could see that someone had advised him as to the approach that would succeed. His performance was quite good and I obliged. I don't know if they ever approached Blaney.

Taca opened with a formal dinner attended to the best of my knowledge by all the members of the government. It immediately caught the imagination of the media and the opposition and many wild rumours were circulated about the dinner and the nature and purpose of the new group. For instance, someone must have heard the figure £100 mentioned and it was described as a Hundred-Pounds-A-Plate Dinner. The opposition parties with the perspicacity which has kept them almost permanently in opposition decided that at last they had the weapon to destroy the enemy. All they had to do was to scream about corruption from the housetops, point to Taca as proof, and the job was done. When will they ever learn? The significance of Taca was not that it was institutionalised corruption as they claimed. It was no such thing. They knew that themselves and could not be convincing in their efforts to get the public to believe it. Corruption is not organised in public and ordinary people would have enough common sense to realise that if there is corruption it is a hole-and-corner affair hidden as securely as possible from the eyes of man. That is if they were interested at all in the possibility of there being corruption and bearing in mind the disinterest in the publicly established infamy of 1970 this must be doubtful. As far as Fianna Fáil were concerned, it was as good a way for the opposition to occupy themselves as any other. I was in charge of a number of Fianna Fáil by-election campaigns while the attempted Taca smear was in full swing and it was a great help to know that the opposition were wasting their time chasing a shadow. It was easy to deal with the campaign. All one had to do was to ignore it. I really believe they even forgot about the personal anti-Haughey rumours until the Arms Non-Crisis gave them a new lease of life. With unerring instinct they had picked Haughey out at the start of his career, when as a young UCD alumnus he was losing his deposit in local government elections, and they were still after him. Now they had us all together. They were soon back to Haughey.

All of the members of Taca had for some years been subscribing at election time substantially more than the total of their between-election Taca subscriptions even if elections were to come only at the full five year intervals. Everyone knew, of course, that they would continue to do so. Certainly Taca was a development of great significance in regard to the character of Fianna Fáil but it had nothing to do with corruption. Its significance was that it unmistakably marked the accelerating change from the small man's party, priding itself on its total dependence on the small subscriptions collected once a year in every parish in the Twenty-six Counties, to a party still using the same type of election worker but now financially patronised by the bosses. For years it had been a proud Fianna Fáil boast that they won elections at a fraction of the cost at which Fine Gael and Labour lost them. A half-crown subscription at the chapel gate was genuinely appreciated more than the first £500 subscription. What Taca established was that the financial support of the entrepreneurial class was very substantial and had become vital and this was a very serious development indeed. The danger seen by a few in the early 1930s had materialised and it seemed to be only a matter of time until this financial dependence would manifest itself in the matter of policy to such an extent that the people would realise there had been a definite shift to the right in Fianna Fáil's political position. Fine Gael had long ago proved that to be widely recognised as the right wing party resulted in being a permanent minorty party. This was the aspect of Taca they should have concentrated on but, of course, this would be difficult since they still had the greater amount of this type of financial support themselves.

There was a new surge of support from entrenched financial interests and others with a vested interest in the divided country at the time of the Arms Crisis. The party needed to be buttressed against any possible coup by the shadowy and largely imaginary group known as dissidents. Satisfied at last that Fianna Fáil had finally divested itself of the taint of Republicanism more of the financial establishment decided to give their support. Their grip began to tighten but it was only in response to the introduction by the Coalition of new taxation on wealth and capital gains that money really began to flow in a flood-tide to Fianna Fáil headquarters. Taca was no more than a natural decision by some people in the business of making money to support a party which had proved in a general way that its system of government produced favourable circumstances for commercial activity, whereas the Coalition had produced the opposite. In any case many of the members of Taca had Republican backgrounds and some had always been supporters from the time, as Blaney remarked, when they hardly had a seat in their pants. The influx induced by the 1973-77 Coalition, however, was of a different nature. It was a headlong panic-stricken rush for self-preservation. It was purely pragmatic with no pretence of idealism involved. These people were making an investment on which they expected a return, and they intended to call the tune. Now, as far as I can gather, many of them have decided that self-preservation requires a change to one of the alternative leaders on offer to the Fianna Fáil faithful. Well that's their business and it is a possibilty that should have been foreseen. It is a fairly well known experience in other countries that the big financial backers are liable to decide to call in the chips when they see their interests are at stake.

The bonanza began to accrue when Fianna Fáil were in opposition and the first priority of the party and its new financial support was to bring about a change in government. The first result was the provision of back-up services to compensate for the non-availability of the civil service. It was a bad decision in more ways than one. For one thing it made the party dependent on this new income and that was, to say the least, dangerous to its freedom in matters of policy. It also meant the end of the old process of ideas seeping upwards from the ordinary members in a vague form through the successive levels of the organisation and eventually influencing policy. Now the party had experts on tap and henceforward the cumainn function would be purely mechanical. For the 1977 election the think-tank made its appearance. I had been staving off the offer of expert advice since 1957, when as honorary secretary and minister I began to come under pressure to devise a way to avail of the technical and academic expertise available in the party to develop policy. I was still kicking to touch when I left in 1970. As I have already mentioned, the result of the think-tank was the 1977 Manifesto and the result of the Manifesto is the economic disaster from which we are suffering. The saddest thing about the Manifesto is that it was completely unnecessary. Apparently the fact that the elements which have been financing the party to a great extent since the 1973-77 Coalition are now threatening to withdraw support, is one of the major factors being interpreted as indicating the imminent electoral decline of Fianna Fáil. The amusing thing about this is that their displeasure arises from the ruination of the economy. This arose from the fact that the government actually decided to try to implement the Manifesto and this document emanated from the think-tank, which was the direct result of their self-preservation investment and which was stupidly briefed to produce a sure-fire election winner rather than a realistic programme for the rescue of the economy in difficult international circumstances. So it was really their own fault. Obviously the withdrawal of the financial support would be serious for a party which has acquired such a complex and sophisticated headquarters and has come to depend on it. If this sudden accretion of money is withdrawn, it may very well result in a decline in the only real terms a pragamtic party understands but it also represents a possible favourable factor in the long term, if by any near-miracle there was a move towards the re-birth of the party. It would not then be hamstrung by the existence in the background of a faceless board of controlling directors. It took a long time for the full effects of the acceptance of the first big cheque to materialise.

III

I suppose that it was only when the 1971 Ard Fheis ratified by resolution not merely the standards of public morality embodied in the November 1970 Motion of Confidence but also the reversal of policy in regard to Partition, that the party can be said with certainty to have lost the sense of national purpose which had motivated it and sustained its morale for so long. Of course, the fact is as in the case of the other aspects of change mentioned, that a change of this magnitude does not occur overnight and this change was probably beginning to take place almost from the start. The situation resulting from the factual establishment of two separate regimes under elected Irish governments in the two artificially defined parts of the country was, as it was intended to be, a situation in which progress towards the realisation of the national aim would be very difficult. In the Six Counties, as far as the section of the national majority coerced out of the Irish State was concerned, it involved continuous non-acceptance of the legitimacy of the regime created by the British parliament for their permanent and unjust coercion. It involved continuous opposition to the national minority who were constituted a permanent majority in the area by the British legislation and the skilfully, maliciously and undemocratically drawn Border. For this dissident minority, it involved a permanent siege mentality and by conferring on them the false status of loyalist, it imposed on them the loyal duty of continuously suppressing the members of the majority in the area. For the whole area it involved permanent sectarian division and discrimination on this basis as surely as if this was a fundamental provision of a written constitution.

In the new Twenty-six County State progress towards the national objective involved what amounted to the subversion of the established State. Since the institutions of the

State were clearly accepted by the people, it followed that it was only through these institutions the national objective could be pursued legitimately. In practical terms this meant that the only justifiable approach was that adopted by Fianna Fáil. The programme, therefore, had to be to go into the Dáil, to become the government and to concentrate as a government on bringing about the end of the circumstances in which they were the government. This was the only feasible approach. The snag was that it was contrary to human nature. From the moment a person took the first step on this programme for achieving the national objective, he or she became subject to a powerful influence tending to corrupt the underlying principle. By 1971, when the moment of truth was starkly presented to them and they decided to change their mind on the 1926 policy, Fianna Fáil were the near permanent government. They had been in office continuously since 1932 with the exception of two short three year interruptions. At the 1971 Ard Fheis the time had come when they could no longer postpone a decision on whether or not the solution of the problem of successfully bringing in the North should be confidently undertaken. They knew exactly what was involved, knew the decision their traditional allegiance called for but, at the previous Ard Fheis, I had reminded them that the achievement of their national objective could conceivably amount to *felo de se* for the party. Taking account of human nature, was it surprising that they decided, under the urging of the leadership, not to take a decison which might result in such a terrible crime?

The two factors favouring the permanence of the *status quo* were the permanent unionist majority built in to the Six County area and the fact that it was only by becoming the dominant force in the political establishment of the Twenty-six Counties that those in favour of undoing this injustice of Partition could undertake that objective. Seán Etchingham's forecast in the Treaty debate was right. From the moment one became a member of the Free State establishment, consciously or unconsciously, one became subject to the debilitating influence of an ever-growing vested interest. If a person was conscious of this, it could be countered in accordance with the strength of character of the person concerned, but if one did not realise this influence was there, it was almost certain to prevail and, of course, no one would know for certain that the vested interest had prevailed until the moment of decision was at hand. It can be taken for granted, then, that among the top, that is the professional echelons of Fianna Fáil there had been a gradual dissipation of the enthusiasm of 1926. Another factor tending to produce the same result was that from the late 1930s onwards Fianna Fáil had to deal with a militant Republican opposition as well as a political Free State or ex-Free State opposition. It requires a continuous realisation of the danger of one's own Republican allegiance being weakened by the suppression of militant Republicanism, to avoid that result. A third factor was the intake of new members over the years of political success who like the then Taoiseach did not seem to know or care too much what Fianna Fáil was all about. The effect of all these factors did not emerge publicly until the actual moment of decision came and by then the small Republican minority of the 1969 government had been eliminated largely through their own supineness. There were, however, indications since the renewal of the baptismal vows in 1951 which should have led to a greater awareness of the potentiality for weakness in the party on the matter of fundamental principle.

When I first became a member of the government in 1957, it was quite clear that the solution to the problem was not being undertaken with any degree of urgency although it had been proclaimed with a fanfare of trumpets, not only in 1951 but also in 1947, that the stage for this effort had been reached. We had, of course, urgent economic and social problems to deal with so, particularly since there was no movement in the Six County area itself, it was not surprising that it was purely a question of rectifying the economic collapse with the vague hope, which was really only an assumed hope, that eventually the Twenty-six Counties would present an attractive prospect to the hardheaded unionists. This seemed no more than apathy arising from the essential concentration on the immediate priority but a little over ten years later, when the Colley Committee on the Constitution published its first and only interim report, it was a different matter.

This printed report, which is on sale through any bookseller and which was signed by six members of the Fianna Fáil party, unanimously proposed to ask the people to withdraw, by referendum, the national claim to the integrity of the nation as a matter of right *(See Appendix C, page 145)*. The ground for the proposal was prepared in the introduction which in listing twelve alleged basic elements of the Constitution omitted the real basic element without batting an eyelid. This was the stating of the national claim to the rightful integrity of the whole of Ireland and it was the principal reason for the 1937 Constitution. It was the most important thing in the Constitution because by this article the people themselves denounced the action of their elected representatives in ratifying the Tripartite Boundary Agreement and, quite clearly, this still rankled with the successors of the old Cumann na nGaedheal who were on the committee. The recommendation was to propose to remove Article 3 and to replace it by an article reducing the re-unification of the country to the status of a mere pious aspiration. This was a proposal engineered by the skilful Coalition team to revert to the Free State position in which the Six Counties entity was ratified by the Twenty-six County parliament. It would, of course, copper-fasten the *status quo* because it would be done by the people not by the minority of the elected representatives who ratified the Boundary Agreement in the absence of the Republican deputies, and it would be a specific reversion from the established position which stated the fact that the division of the Irish nation was not accepted. This was a clear and most serious indication of the extent of the defection from the initial Republican principles of the party in the ranks of the parliamentary tier. I warned the party publicly as clearly as I felt I could while remaining a member of the government. I circulated the text of a speech which was deliberately very short so that the import of it could not be misconstrued if it was reported at all. It was reported. None of the media knew what I was talking about, obviously because neither political correspondents nor editors had read the report, but I was gradually spreading the word of what was in it to members of the organisation. The matter was not decided. It was still hanging fire. I raised the matter immediately at government level and intended to do so again up to the time I left two and a half years later. I had put the Taoiseach on notice at a meeting of the government of my intention. As far as I was concerned, this report was something I was not going to stand for. I intended to insist on its rejection by the government and if this meant the resignation of either myself or Mr Colley that was something that could not be avoided. Probably the most disturbing thing about this was that there was no ground swell in the organisation, but then Fianna Fáil members are like newspaper political correspondents and editors — they read only the headlines. As well as that, they were long accustomed to trusting the leadership implicitly in these matters. I, certainly, was not surprised when in 1969 Mr Colley emerged as the leader of the majority faction in the government which opted for the new principle 'to preserve at all costs what we have achieved down here'. What we had achieved was virtually permanent jobs as government ministers in the context of the partitioned situation or as Pearse put it, 'We had gained all things, land and good living and the friendship of our foe.' The recent Colley-Kelly axis, with the Fine Gael partner issuing the hit-list of Fianna Fáil undesirables who must go when the saints come marching in, also seems a natural development from the 1967 alignment to revert to the Free State position on Partition.

Since 1970 Fianna Fáil's new bi-partisan, or Cumann na nGaedheal, policy has developed from the initial sabotaging of the Citizen's Defence Committees and the tacit withdrawal of the old claim that 'the gravest injury which one nation can inflict upon another' should be undone in the British parliament where it was perpetrated in the first place, to the comprehensive alliance between the Irish government and Her Majesty's government. Throughout all this period, there have been people in Fianna Fáil who were able to convince themselves they were fighting from within to redeem the party from this great shame. They certainly displayed an amazing capacity to keep a stiff upper lip while one step after another was taken in developing the complete participation of our institutions with the British military repression of the Irish loyalists. They consoled themselves with dark mutterings in darker corners and with assuring people like myself, when they could get us to listen to their pathetic self-exculpation, that the dawning of the day was approaching inexorably, day by day and year by year.

Without any evidence discernible to an outside observer, without a solitary public word from the principal, there has been a well orchestrated rumour that this great in-fighting movement, the only Irish political movement that ever succeeded in keeping its activities and manipulations completely hidden from the public eye, was being brilliantly directed by the master strategist, Mr C. J. Haughey. How anyone could believe that beats me. Mr Haughey was interpreted as throwing down the gauntlet after his acquittal in the Arms Trial. If so, he had it well retrieved and safely pocketed again before the then Taoiseach returned from America. I don't believe he himself could possibly have believed he was fighting from within during the next ten degrading years. What he was doing was publicly grovelling at the feet of his traducers and letting his manhood drain away year by humiliating year, waiting for the effluxion of time to demolish his enemy and relying on the ever-faithful media to ensure without any help from him, that he was the 'Republican alternative'. I suppose the people who had to find something to believe in order to retain some degree of self-esteem are not to be blamed for accepting the fantasy that they were members of a great movement, brilliantly led by a man from whom they never heard — not a word. When the deed was done it was they who had done it! Now the line of national advance could be resumed after ten years of collaboration with the repressive regime of the British army, the modern Black and Tans, and after upwards of two thousand deaths, due to Fianna Fáil defection. They had placed their own chosen leader at their head and everything would be all right from now on. No need now for the dark conspiratorial attitude. The day had dawned in Erin and from now on they could 'Step together, boldly tread, Firm each foot, erect each head.' By now they see that the pace of increasing collaboration has accelerated to the point where Her Majesty's writ runs again in the whole of Ireland, enforced here by our institutions, in other words by the people. Where can they turn now? What more could they have done than replace the false prophet by the man the media told them was the 'Republican alternative' and whose sincerity and dedication was authenticated by one spectacular incident, by the fact that he had been charged with the heinous offence of attempting to import arms illegally? His denial of involvement in any way had, it is true, been accepted, or so it appeared to most observers, but the aura had been acquired in the same historic court where so many an ever-lasting patriotic aura had been acquired in somewhat similar circumstances. It was just that he was more fortunate than his illustrious predecessors — he was acquitted. Fianna Fáil had long ago renounced the gunmen but this was the next best thing, the shadow of a gunman.

Mr de Valera gave potent reasons, in 1926, why it was not feasible to fight from within Sinn Féin for a realistic and justifiable policy in the new circumstances of the time, and I gave equally potent reasons from 1971 why it was not feasible to fight from within Fianna Fáil, when the Ard Fheis had endorsed the reversal of policy already implemented by the divinely appointed leadership. I didn't fight from within Fianna Fáil and neither did anyone else. Those who believed they remained to fight from within have found themselves having to stand idly by while this generation of the Irish people were weaned away from the old allegiance over a long period during which the death toll was mounting. This was because when the media told them they had a dynamic and brilliant leader within the walls they accepted it, although the nominated one never told them what was happening or what they should do. Yet surely they must have known that the reason it was not possible to fight from within Fianna Fáil was that anyone who attempted to lead against the leadership would be most effectively and expeditiously liquidated? They could not be led from within and they would not be led from without and so all they could do was watch in impotence while collaboration became more and more complete until the two security forces, or is it three, can now be seen by anyone to 'proceed along parallel lines and in a common direction so that the resultant of their combined efforts may be the greatest possible.' Mrs Thatcher is satisfied. Further proof of the completeness of our involvement is not necessary. The lady is displeased with us only over Las Malvinas and this was engineered to mollify the surviving Republican backwoodsmen.

Fianna Fáil policy was reversed as soon as the circumstances in the Six Counties made it really relevant for the first time, because members who knew what was happening and who claimed they disagreed with it allowed it to happen and for no other reason. It is all right to blame Mr Lynch but he didn't know any better. They did but, misinterpreting their duty as soldiers of destiny, they clicked their heels and said, 'Yes, sir' to directions they knew to be wrong and dutifully joined in the standing ovations when the cheer-leaders gave them the nod. They stood idly by, they did not fight from within, while their army joined in Operation Motorman, sealing off possible lines of escape while Free Derry was being annihilated, while the defensive barriers in other nationalist areas were swept away and while a British striking force was once more established in the Republic of South Armagh. The cynical, opportunistic attendance of a few members of the government at the funerals of the victims of our British army paratroop allies assuaged whatever degree of anger they may have felt at the Bloody Sunday murders in Derry. They tolerated the continuous development of the alliance, while CS gas and plastic bullets were being widely and indiscriminately used against their kith and kin. They condoned the killing of innocent people, young and old, by the allied security forces. They allowed their government to accept passively Mrs Thatcher's exacting of her pound of flesh by insisting on the deaths of ten hunger-strikers who by any test were political prisoners. They raised no objection while the Offences against the State Act was amended to provide, among other things, that a person could make a subversive statement by nodding his head or applauding at the wrong time and that a person could be convicted on the unsupported opinion of a garda officer, who could have this opinion without ever having seen the accused person in his life until he saw him in the dock. The bombs in Dublin city that ensured the passage of the amendment were accepted like everything else without protest as an operation in the common cause of making the croppies lie down. British intelligence operations in the Twenty-six Counties, Wyman, Crinnion, the Littlejohns to name only a few, as well as SAS activity in the State, did not shake their belief that their sole guiding principle must continue to be unquestioning allegiance to the leader. The fact is that the whole process of increasing collaboration was unanimous.

Now the man they have been led to believe was their leader in the fight from within has been elected to replace Mr Lynch. They find that while there has been the first unobjectionable visit to America by an Irish leader for over a decade and while there has been an unconvincing coolness with the British government about an island on the other side of the world, at the same time our participation in the British military campaign in our own country has become even more intense, and they claim to be bemused. 'How can this be? He was supposed to be our man.' They see a virtual breakdown of law and order in the Twenty-six Counties. Shopkeepers and private householders can almost tell from the pattern of robberies in their area that they are nearing the head of the housebreakers' list but they know there is nothing they can do about it. They know that the simple fact is that there is no protection available. The gardaí cannot be in two places at the same time. They know that when the crimes are committed there will be no detection. Except for major crimes like murder, detectives are for the support of the British regime in our country, part of the national drive to ensure that the British army are not hampered in their historic and perennial task of solving the Irish Question. The priority in regard to the limited prison space available is for those whose conviction arises from what used to be the never-failing source of all our political evils. If the housebreakers, the muggers, the violent armed robbers were apprehended and convicted, there would be undue pressure on the prison accommodation required by the British alliance. They know that the courts which are already too busy to deal with anything like reasonable expedition with matters seriously affecting the people who pay for the administration of justice, now have to find time to deal without delay with offences against Her Majesty's peace alleged to have been committed within the territory of the United Kingdom in Armagh and Belfast and Derry (sorry, Londonderry). How can the people of Tallaght expect more than a derisory garda presence to prevent spectacular armed raids worthy of the infamous James brothers in their hey-day when they are paying as much as they can pay to provide as many gardaí as Mrs Thatcher requires for Border co-operation? How can postmasters and postal delivery men expect to be protected from armed attack when the gardaí, whose wages they pay, are on the Border ensuring that British army snatch gangs are not molested by the outraged citizens of towns on our side of the Border, and escorting detachments of Her Majesty's soldiery back to the bosoms of their commanding officers with their illegally imported arms intact? How can people expect to be reasonably safe from being mugged in our cities, when the primary function of the garda síochana is to guard the rear of the British army in the Six Counties?

We cannot have it both ways. We can pay for our own protection or for the protection of Her Majesty's forces but it is beyond our capacity to pay for both. The people willingly contribute their money for the latter purpose. In doing so they opt to forego their own protection and it is illogical to complain when they are not protected. They have no cause for complaint if it is only a matter of time until their houses are burgled, and if Fianna Fáil members want to know how this situation came about the answer is simple. It is because they acquiesced at all stages in the development of the total alliance with the British military effort in the Six Counties. Fianna Fáil is now clearly a 'government under contract with the enemy to maintain his overlordship' in the Six Counties, in a direct manner un-

dreamt of even in 1926 when Mr Eamon de Valera used
these words in talking of the first Free Staters.

This is the real decline of Fianna Fáil although it cannot
be divorced from the other aspects mentioned which are all
part of the total degeneration of the party. There are, of
course, party members who are genuinely asking, 'How did
it happen? What happened to our great movement which
we were told was fighting from within? We changed leaders,' people say in mystification, 'and Mr Haughey seemed
to have the qualifications and still we find ever more complete collaboration.' They genuinely don't like being in the
British camp. They know in their bones that when a British
army is in their country on a war-footing in support of the
British jurisdiction in Ireland they should not be with them,
but they are with them and it is their own fault. They have
paid the price of allowing themselves to be ruled for too
long by the old, illogical, undemocratic and moronic taboo
— the leader is inviolate and his whim is our policy — and if
now they have no one to whom they can turn to rescue
them from their shameful position, that is their own fault
too. They, the ordinary, unpaid members stuck with the
leader who when challenged on the blatant reneging of the
fundamental party principle which they knew was a fact,
was backed by the parliamentary party, the elite. This was
enough for them. When eventually the parliamentary party
turned on him for ignoble personal motives the ordinary
members again followed suit blindly, and now they are
impotent. The alternatives on offer have one thing in common, they all present a worse prospect.

The principle of loyalty to the leader though the heavens
fall, which is not a virtue, has been probably the cardinal
principle of Fianna Fáil since its inception. Fianna Fáil was
a split in Sinn Féin. There must never be another split. So
most of the few who could not stomach the British alliance
just quietly folded their tents and slipped away out of the
political scene. This perverse principle of unconditional
loyalty to an individual rather than to a national policy,
which is really a mark of weakness, indicating a party of
people conditioned not to think for themselves but to act as
automatons, had over-ridden both national and moral prin-

ciple since 1970. It had to a certain extent substituted for the genuine worthy principles of the party, the knowledge that every ignominy had to be accepted for the sake of loyalty, thus helping to maintain some degree of morale in their shame. They excused their defection from real principle, enshrined in their constitution, on the unsustainable ground that loyalty to the man at the top was the supreme requirement to which everything else must be subordinated. Some almost regarded themselves as having acted heroically in enduring stoically self-imposed mortification of the spirit by subordinating their real principles to this over-riding duty of loyalty. Major de Valera, for instance, a brilliant man, who unfortunately insisted on playing soldiers all his life, regarded himself as having the soldierly duty to carry out the dictates of his superiors without question. Did anyone ever hear such nonsense? He was far too intelligent not to know that many of his superiors in rank were very much his inferiors in fact. Their superior rank in the party arose from the fact that his father did not want anyone to think he was trying to establish a dynasty. When, at last, the chosen one was ousted, it was not for national or moral principle. These had already been sacrificed on the false altar of loyalty. The palace revolution was for the sordid motive of saving their own bacon. Then every vestige of self-esteem was gone because at that stage loyalty was all that remained to give solace to their outraged souls.

A once proud, idealistic and disciplined party has degenerated into a miserable, unprincipled and leaderless rabble, a party that demonstrates its own chronic instability with every political wind that blows, incongruously pleading to be allowed to provide stable government, while the leader leads in the knowledge that he is surrounded by colleagues ready to pounce if he makes one false step. He knows that Fianna Fáil hands are rubbed in glee at every minor discomfiture with which he is afflicted. So notwithstanding the fact that both recent general elections and the latest by-elections in Dublin West and East Galway continue to show electoral support maintained at the constant post-1932 level, there has been a catastrophic decline in real terms in the Fianna Fáil party. Can the actual fall, in pragmatic terms, be far away?

10

Hope Springs Eternal

What would the young man today, with strong national feelings, honest and courageous, but without set prejudices or any commitments of his past to hamper him, who aimed solely at serving the national cause and bringing it to a successful issue see? Examining the situation he would see, as his grandfather saw in 1926, to begin with, the country partitioned, North (strictly north-east) separated from South (strictly north and south). The only difference now would be that he would have a further fifty-six years of the experience of this injustice to contemplate. What else would he see? He would see the full capacity of the legal and security forces at the disposal of the elected government ranged side by side with the legal and security forces of the foreign master in defence of that partition. Would he not then conclude that the political parties, and in particular the Fianna Fáil party had, in fact, succumbed to the sixty years of Free State fat in their bodies?

What advice should I give such a young man? I have already futilely proferred the advice given to me in February 1971 by my father, the most forceful advocate of the 1926 New Departure and the principal constructor of Fianna Fáil, to accept that it was in the nature of things that when they reach the top they must decay and that it was now time to start a new party. Many honest and courageous young men had seen the disastrous collapse of a slightly constitutional party in the hour of need and they were not disposed to destine themselves now to an even longer wait for their tyrants to suffer a change of heart. It has been suggested to me that I should now advise an attempt to re-form Fianna Fáil by joining it. This is the advice to stay and work from within which de Valera so quickly rejected in 1925, because he saw clearly that the group led and typified by Mary MacSwiney would never yield one inch. It is the advice I rejected in 1971 because no one knew the appallingly low calibre of the parliamentary party better than I. I knew nothing could be accomplished with that material and since then the quality of the material has gone down and down and down until it has reached the abyss of the two (or three or four) sickening factions so starkly demonstrated in the aftermath of the 1982 election. It must be clear that reform would require as a first step a virtually new parliamentary group and how could this be accomplished from within? The honest and courageous young men and women would have to unseat the incumbents, beat them at their own game, the game they have perfected — intrigue and organisational manipulation. A long process! And I who have seen this process in action cannot visualise initial personal idealism surviving a long process of wheeling and dealing in order to overcome expert and long-experienced practitioners in the art of wheeling and dealing. Indeed, I cannot see the idealist succeeding against the unprincipled pragmatist, particularly when the latter is well-heeled, except by open and direct confrontation. The young man, honest and courageous, against the old man and the young men with the mohair suits and the entrepreneurial financial backing in an organisation tailored to the materialistic and permissive society — it seems to me that reform from inside is too much to expect!

Pearse would recognise a period where some brave man would be needed to redeem us with a sacrifice. Possibly there is still hope here, but there have been sacrifices and the public verdict appears to be that self-sacrifice at any level is an indication of foolishness, immaturity, incapacity to move with the times and personal unsuitability for the political game which is intrinsically for unscrupulous pragmatists. In Ireland sacrifice has ensured the survival of the cause for future generations but only rarely has it had an immediate effect. The hunger-strike deaths may appear to have been futile, but if the rearguard action of the professional politicians does succeed in postponing the British withdrawal for another generation, they will have the traditional effect. Maybe the experience, which seems likely in the future, of one group of political pragmatists after another submitting themselves as governments to the veto of tiny minorities opposed to all our traditions will eventually rouse the people to turn on the time-servers on whom they have relied for too long. Maybe the continued attrition of the British resolve to resist the inevitable withdrawal from Ireland by the dogged determination and resilience of the IRA will eventually cause the professional politicians in both parts of Ireland to decide to get on the bandwagon before it is too late.

Hope there must be. A struggle which in various forms has persisted for eight hundred years, is not going to peter out with the goal in sight and with British imperialism gone everywhere else except in Las Malvinas and Gibraltar and a few minor dots on the globe that everyone has forgotten. There is, however, no reason to hope in an uncleansed Fianna Fáil. Just as hope in O'Connell died with the defeat at Clontarf, hope in Fianna Fáil died with the 1971 Ard Fheis. After all the centuries the Irish people must know in their hearts that the present attitude of participation in the British effort to impose a military solution cannot survive. I cannot pretend to foretell how the change will come. I put forward the obvious solution and it was rejected. Maybe it was badly timed and inadequately prepared but with violence developing as it was it is still my opinion that it was then the option of non-violence, withdrawn by Fianna Fáil's defection, was necessary. If it was not taken that could not be helped. There was no one else to make the effort to fill the vacuum in constitutional politics and for twelve years there has been no alternative to the violent method of which Mr de Valera had said at the first Ard Fheis of Fianna Fáil, 'in history it is seldom that foreign tyrants have yielded to any other'.

I tried to warn the still surviving Republican element in Fianna Fáil earlier, in the context of the publicly proposed sell-out in the Report of the Colley Committee. I can do no more. In the moment of truth the organisation was totally dominated by the doctrine of leadership infallibility, and of unquestioning loyalty to the current wearer of the mantle of de Valera. It was not part of their function to question the personal qualifications of the leader or any of his actions. He was the successor appointed by the elected representatives. Therefore, if to a lowly cumann member his actions, measured either by a Republican or ethical yardstick, appeared dubious, this was merely an indication of the naîvety of those who had no access to the corridors of power. How could a small farmer, a national teacher or a mere urban worker expect to comprehend these things? So in the 1960s and 1970s the Republicans could not be warned but now the elected representatives themselves have created a new situation where the head that wears the crown lies uneasily; where the crown is always up for grabs in government, out of government and before, during and after general elections and by-elections; where the leader is the prime target for character assassination by the party faithful in the pub after the cumann meeting and even on the voters' doorsteps. Maybe the time is coming when a cleansing is at last feasible. The question is from where is the person to lead such a movement to come? Well, that is for today's young man setting out on the line of national advance to decide. If such a young man decides he should join the same party his predecessor joined in 1926, then let him look around for a leader and get him or her to join with him. There is no such person in the existing party.

The absence of anyone with a genuine commitment to the old ideals of the 1926 line of national advance and not involved in the abandoning of the principle of integrity in public life is a serious matter not only for the party as such but for the nation as a whole. It means that there is no existing medium through which this generation of the Irish people can be redeemed from the ignoble position in which their professional politicians have placed them. There is no doubt that the majority of the people do not want their national aspiration to be promoted by the methods of the Provisional IRA, but this does not mean that they do not have this aspiration and that they do not realise that peace in Ireland and goodwill between the people of Ireland and Britain require the ending of the British dimension in Ireland. The tragedy is that the degeneration of Fianna Fáil has betrayed them.

The present economic disaster is, as I have pointed out,

also the result of the change in the character of Fianna Fáil. After about ten years of continuous economic recklessness in government it is not surprising if people are asking how the situation can be rectified under the present system of Fianna Fáil and the Coalition, with a tiny left-wing group, or even the Labour party, exercising a power totally out of proportion to their support in the country.

Where will the courage and determination to tackle it come from? How will the people be inspired to accept hardship and a reduced standard of living for the welfare of the nation, of posterity? Who will stand up to the Herrenvolk of the EEC, our European overlords and say, 'This is our country, these are our people and we will not see them sacrificed to the greed of foreign capitalists?' Who can regenerate the spirit of self-sacrifice of the western small farmers who stood firm while their calves were slaughtered rather than concede to the foreign enemy? In a word, where is the new messiah who can appeal with credibility for the spirit of sacrifice for the common good, who can lead with credibility towards moral regeneration?

It is not necessary to discuss the several individuals reputed to be on offer to come to the conclusion that there is no one within Fianna Fáil capable of doing what is required. They committed the sacrilege of ousting the duly-appointed successor of the founder once. It is true there was a very good reason at the time — their jobs were in danger. This is a once-only operation which can be repeated only at the risk of disintegration. If they now decide they have made a mistake, there is no simple straightforward solution. It is unreasonable and unrealistic to expect the public to wait patiently while Fianna Fáil go through a long process of trial-and-error to find a leader. To admit a second mistake so soon would be to undermine their remaining credibility with the public completely. If the current crop of dissidents believe the replacement has been a failure, what can they do about it? There would have to be someone who would receive virtually unanimous endorsement as the person who could redeem and restore the party. In fact, the only prospect if the present leader is replaced is a period of internal strife leading to significant disruption and to deterioration if not, indeed, to total disintegration. All the pretenders to the crown are tainted in some way or other with the events and trends which brought the party to what it is — the arms crisis, the adoption of Cumann na nGaedheal policy, the alignment with big business, the think-tank as an usurper of the organisation in the matter of policy development, the Manifesto, not to mention the many diverse and possibly minor incidents which added together constitute the moral decline following inevitably from the formal adoption of the standards of the arms trial. The known aspirants to the succession are all more closely implicated in the Manifesto, the immediate source of the ruination of the economy, than is the present Taoiseach. There is no one among the older hands or the younger whizz kids who has at any time given any indication of a personal wish to be aligned with the traditional approach to the injustice of Partition and to the British aggression of continuing to insist on the retention of part of the Irish nation within the Union. If there are, in fact, people in the party who recognise its present sordidness and who really want to see it redeemed, it is obvious that they must be prepared to look outside the party for a redeemer.

Throughout the whole period from 1969, my consideration of the position, my 'appreciation of the line of possible national advance' has always amounted to the one sentence — the British must decide to go — to such an extent that I always think of Cato the Elder, who is reputed to have ended his every speech in the Roman senate with *Carthago delenda est*. Every other way but this has been tried. So there is no other way. From 1971 I have also felt compelled to say with equal monotony, Fianna Fáil must be replaced. If I could now say with any degree of hope that Fianna Fáil must be reformed from within I would say it, but with my knowledge of the personnel involved and the public presentation of the new acquisitions, whom I do not know, this seems to me to be out of the question. As I see it the best prospect is that the warring factions will turn on one another and tear the party asunder. If so, there will be a disastrous period of reaction and despair but there will also be the required cleansing from which a movement may emerge to take the last step.

Fianna Fáil's rise as the Republican party brought the national advance to the penultimate stage. Should there have been a new assessment of the situation at that point, a new projected line of national advance, bearing in mind the sudden adherence of all political parties to the taking of the final step? Was Fianna Fáil on its own no longer the appropriate instrument? The obstacle to a unified national effort at home was gone, but maybe the national effort had come to be regarded as the sole property of a political party. This was understandable but may have been disastrous. Certainly Fianna Fáil's decline as the Republican party manifested from 1969 has extended the period of Ireland's martyrdom and it appears it will be further unnecessarily extended as the party's internal stresses are sorted out. What about it? The problem has been with us for eight hundred years. In 1969 we were starting on the ninth century. Maybe we would be lost without it.

'Hope springs eternal in the human breast' and, bad as things are, I don't see the need for despair. Is it for a miracle I hope? Possibly, but the miraculous regeneration of Fianna Fáil seems too much to hope for involving as it must a spectacular change of personnel at the top. The more realistic hope seems to be that the deterioration in the national position will create a climate favourable for a new idealism and a new leader to sweep away the utter sordidness that has developed from the appalling reaction to the new situation in the Six Counties and that, when that day comes, a new leader will be available. The essential thing is, I believe, that the people themselves will decide to regenerate public life, to reject the standards adopted by the Dáil in 1970 and applied with disastrous results since, and also to insist that the solution of the final problem be confidently undertaken as was promised. Otherwise the inevitable future is the continued, violent attrition of the British resolve to continue with the perpetration of the injustice of 1920 and 1925. Surely it is not too much to hope that after fourteen years of continuous physical violence we are approaching the stage where the Irish people will say —

Hold, Enough! and reject violence in the only way this can be done effectively, by deciding that the time has come to secure by massive peaceful pressure from the Irish race at home and abroad a British commitment to complete the withdrawal from Ireland? That is all that is needed and it is all that was needed in 1969 when the opportunity was there to get a bi-partisan policy based on the unanimous Dáil and Séanad Resolution passed in the time of the first Coalition. The climate of Irish and international public opinion was ideal for such a peaceful Irish initiative from August 1969 onwards until the Fianna Fáil betrayal of the Citizens Defence Committees. If people who see the need for this believe the best thing is to join Fianna Fáil in the hope of being there for the dawning of the day, who am I to try to dissuade them? The point, however, is that a revival cannot be engineered from inside working with the present material. The only possibility is a sudden surge to a new messiah coming from outside. That may appear to be a prospect so remote as not to merit consideration. Still, in his *Diread,* Hugh Mac Diarmaid says: 'The inaccessible pinnacle is not inaccessible', but then he was only a poet like Davis and Pearse and Yeats, who wrote rubbish about 'A Nation Once Again', 'The Risen People' and 'Four Green Fields'. Be that as it may, the Irish-British situation is an anachronism in the modern world. Surely it cannot survive? It must end some time and there is no way it can end except in the breaking of the British connection and the consequent development of the special relationship, which is the underlying reality in the bogus United Kingdom. What a tragedy that at the critical moment Fianna Fáil, de Valera's party, opted out of the leadership of the national advance and sold us all down the drain.

Postscript

The unexpected general election of November 1982 has created a new situation, which calls for some examination in the context of this book. The result was, Fianna Fáil 75, Fine Gael 70, Labour 16, Workers Party 2, Independents 3 (including the Ceann Comhairle). In the light of thirty-four unbroken years of Fine Gael–Labour Coalition in government and opposition, the result has been universally interpreted as a defeat for Fianna Fáil. It is true that, shortly before the defeat of the Fianna Fáil government formed after the February 1982 election, the annual conference of the Labour party decided there should not be a coalition arrangement before the next general election, but this has happened before and past experience justifies the assumption that this decision was merely a matter of election tactics.

This time the state of the economy is even more critical than in the spring of the year, when the new government was constructed on the basis of a massive financial deal for Dublin city contracted with a single independent deputy. Almost everyone appears to accept that a period of single-minded, determined and responsible handling of the economy is essential, yet it is known that the bargaining is to consist of the marrying of two opposing policies — surely an even more dangerous process than the expensive molification of a single individual. There can be no doubt that this is exactly what the people voted for. It emerged clearly during the February 1982 election campaign that the Fianna Fáil and Fine Gael approach to the remedying of the economic crisis, for which they were both responsible, was virtually the same. The trouble was that neither party was allowed to carry out the corrective measures they believed to be necessary. It was also clear from the election results that the vast majority of the people believed their approach was necessary. In November 1982 Fianna Fáil (including Neil Blaney) needed a minimum of one extra seat for an overall majority while Fine Gael needed a minimum of twenty. (This is on the assumption that the Ceann Comhairle's position was not changed.) Obviously the best chance of the necessary corrective action being consistently applied lay in a marginal swing to Fianna Fáil. At best Fine Gael would continue to be dependent on the Labour party support. Very few people could have had any doubt about that. Yet the floating vote decided to attempt the impossible. There was no deceit and, rightly or not, it is regarded as a foregone conclusion that Fine Gael–Labour negotiations will be successful — that is, of course, in so far as the oscillation of ministerial status and Mercedes cars is concerned. There is no discussion on whether the infusion of some elements of Labour policy into the Fine Gael matrix is the required prescription to cure our grievous economic ills. Presumably this will come up for discussion in 1986 or 1987. What I am concerned with here is the implications of the election result and of the events leading up to it in regard to the decline of Fianna Fáil in qualitative and quantitative terms.

I have already referred to the manner in which the necessary support for the Fianna Fáil government formed in March 1982 was obtained. It involved the pre-empting of large amounts of capital finance for a number of projects, most if not all of which were justified in themselves but which almost certainly would not have qualified for immediate sanction if they had to be considered in the normal way in competition with all the other claims for the limited total amount available. Apart from the plausible argument that the allocation of capital in this way, before the Dáil had even met for the first time, militated against the prospect of the rehabilitation of the economy — the manner in which the decisions were made ensured that the personalised campaign against the Fianna Fáil leader would continue after the election. There was no let-up by the media. The disaffected members of the party were constantly encouraged in their disaffection. The subscribers, as distinct from the members began to say, one to the other, that there would be no more subscriptions until there was a change of leader. This is the kind of thing that snowballs.

The government struggled through the budget and other financial business and seized with relief the breathing space of the summer adjournment. But the media had to be saying something during this period and 'Haughey must go' became the prevailing cliché. Still, it was only a few months since the effort to topple the leader had failed miserably and it came as an undoubted surprise when Deputy McCreevy announced with a fanfare of trumpets that he was proposing a Vote of No-Confidence in Mr Haughey at a party meeting before the re-opening of the Dáil. Mr Haughey's response was that this time the challenge must go ahead; the dissidents must stand up and be counted in a roll-call vote. There was an outcry from the principals in the parliamentary party and their media godfathers saying it was a breach of fundamental democratic principle forsooth. Did anyone ever hear such nonsense? These were not anonymous ordinary citizens exercising the franchise. They were public representatives elected under Mr Haughey's leadership proposing to remove him half a year after they had unanimously supported him as Taoiseach. This was a serious proposition affecting the public interest. It is certainly a fundamental democratic principle that election ballots are secret but it is also a fundamental democratic principle that elected public representatives vote publicly on matters affecting the public. Otherwise how can the electorate carry out their democratic function correctly? How can they decide in a responsible way how to vote the next time? So city councillors, county councillors, urban councillors, town commissioners and TDs vote publicly. In fact, even senators who are not really elected public representatives at all vote publicly. This was a case of members of the Taoiseach's political party expressing no-confidence in him. Not alone was every member of the political party concerned entitled to know how every member of the parliamentary party voted but every member of the electorate was entitled to have the same information. It was their democratic right, essential for the proper functioning of the democratic process. Secret voting in elections and public voting by public representatives are both equally essential features of a democracy. We were told members would not vote publicly the way they would vote in secret. (This is undoubtedly true — I remember pointing this out myself twelve years ago.) But what a commentary this is on the quality of TDs! Surely any such person is unfit to be a public representative and his or her opinions are of no value? The unfortunate thing from the democratic aspect is that neither the open nor the secret method of voting would identify these cravens to the public. In one case they would be afraid to vote the way they wanted to vote, while in the other case they would get away with their cowardice and their votes would count the same as those of genuine public representatives. Instead of sympathising with these poor souls the media would be better employed in trying to identify them so that their constituents could replace them with more worthy people. In the event, twenty-two deputies stood up and were counted. Mr John Kelly TD of Fine Gael now had the names of twenty-two 'decent' Fianna Fáil TDs for his grand coalition. He shouldn't worry about not having the names of others who would have been decent provided their constituents didn't know about it. They are without any merit whatsoever and are no loss to any cause.

This further exposure of the parliamentary party emphasised the over-all sordidness that had been revealed after the February general election. The general impression created was that they were even worse than had already been shown. The episode did, however, produce a decisive verdict on the question of the leadership and it was clear that at organisation level support for the *status quo* was even more decisive. The outcome appeared to indicate that the internal opposition was discredited and that the future trend would be towards consolidation rather than disruption, but as events turned out there was to be no time for this development to get under way. Ever since the formation of the government in March 1982, Mr Haughey had been harassed by a series of events which, although they did not involve him personally, nevertheless weakened his standing one way or another. As well as this the economic chickens hatched by the 1977 Manifesto, with which he was not personally connected, were coming home to roost with a vengeance. Everyone in the Dáil and the State knew that hairshirt policies were inevitable if the economy was to survive but this did not mean that these policies, when implemented, were going to find widespread acceptance. It was clear that the prospect of the government surviving its next budget was very doubtful. Everything depended on the continued effectiveness of the 'Gregory Deal'. But Mr Haughey's run of ill-luck had not ended. Three more events in rapid succession combined to bring about the general election at a most unpropitious time. Deputy Loughnane of Clare died suddenly. This left the government dependent on both Mr Gregory's and the Ceann Comhairle's votes until the party voting strength could be restored in a by-election. Then, on the day of Deputy Loughnane's funeral, the news broke of a further depletion of voting strength. Deputy Gibbons was seriously ill. Now, the government had not sufficient support to survive a contentious issue when the Dáil resumed for the winter session. Next came the deciding factor. Following the decision by the annual conference of the Labour party to prevaricate on the coalition issue, the leader Mr O'Leary resigned and defected to Fine Gael. Now, both Fianna Fáil with twenty-two dissidents publicly known, with one TD deceased and one seriously ill, and Labour with a lost leader were in disarray. It was the moment of opportunity for Fine Gael and they went for the kill by tabling a Motion of No-Confidence in the government for the opening of the new session. Fianna Fáil dithered in the hope that Labour would not co-operate with their senior partner's decision to capitalise on the suddenly weakened positions of both friend and foe. There was just a chance they might decide to abstain on the pragmatic grounds that the circumstances were not suitable for them but there were other tactical considerations which prevailed and the government was defeated.

At first glance the election result may appear to indicate the beginning of the long-heralded downward plunge of Fianna Fáil in terms of electoral support. This may prove to be so but it is by no means clear and it is certainly not indicated by the actual figures, particularly taking all the circumstances into account. The Coalition clearly have the numbers to last for a full period of four to five years if nothing untoward happens. In this event, Fianna Fáil's post-1932 record of being the only option for stability in government will be shattered. On the other hand they will have four years to pull themselves together, if this can be done and this is very doubtful. A closer look at the election result does not confirm that there has been an unprecedented decline in the party's performance at the polls. On the contrary, in view of their state of disintegration they have done remarkably well.

It is true that the results since 1977 show not alone that Fianna Fáil have developed a downward momentum but, more significantly, that Fine Gael have developed a rising momentum. Obviously it will not be easy to reverse these trends. My personal opinion is that the present parliamentary tier of the party has not got the calibre required for the task unless the new Coalition is as disastrous as its predecessors. As they stand the results show that, in the most difficult of circumstances, Fianna Fáil have succeeded in getting 45.18% of the Dáil seats (slightly more if the position of the Ceann Comhairle is taken into account) with the same percentage of the first preference votes (45.2%). This is the first time the party has not got some advantage, however slight, from the electoral system and this, of course, is a reflection of polarisation for or against Fianna Fáil. It can be pointed out that Fianna Fáil's support, as measured by the electoral system, was lower (44.22%) in 1954 than in November 1982 and that, after three years of Coalition, the party came back with 53.06% of the Dáil seats and stayed for sixteen years.

Can this happen again?

In 1954 there was no disunity, no loss of morale, self-respect or confidence and there were no knives at the ready behind the leader's back. On paper the task of recovery is by no means daunting. For instance, there were fifteen constituencies in which at the end of the count Fianna Fáil had more than two-thirds of the quota of votes needed to obtain an extra seat. Four of these are three seat constituencies, five are four seaters and six are five seaters. The three seaters are Cork South-West, Dublin North, Kerry South and Tipperary North. It is hardly realistic to expect two out of three in Cork South-West but in the other three cases the extra seat is obtainable, if the internal factors in the organisation operating against this can be overcome. The four seat constituencies are Clare, Dublin South-East, Longford-Westmeath, Sligo-Leitrim and Wicklow. In two of these, Dublin South-East and Wicklow, the task is merely to get two out of the four seats and even at the present level of support there is no reason why this should not be achieved even in the Dublin consti- tuency. In the other three the task is to get three out of four. Normally this is virtually impossible to achieve but in Clare it is purely a question of whether the divisive features in this election can be overcome. In Sligo-Leitrim it is largely a question of obtaining a full quota in Leitrim and Fine Gael's handling of the Six County and 'security' situ- ation should produce the missing votes here before the next election. In Longford-Westmeath the third seat is hardly a realistic proposition unless some fortuitous advantage happens to accrue from the two county position. The five seaters are Carlow-Kilkenny, Dublin South-Central, Dun Laoire, Kildare, Limerick East and Wexford. In two of these, Dublin South-Central, and Dun Laoire, the present position is that Fianna Fáil have only one out of five. This, of course, is a ridiculous situation which cannot be ascribed to the actual level of obtainable support. In Dublin South- Central the Ceann Comhairle was returned automatically so that for practical purposes it was a four seater. Fianna Fáil had more than sufficient votes to get two out of five. Only the most exceptional circumstances could result in only one seat out of five even in 'Kingstown' and these cir- cumstances obtained on this occasion. With the official organisation and the outgoing deputies openly opposed to the party leadership it was futile to expect realistic support. This also applies to Limerick East where a semblance of a party-type approach would have produced the third seat. In Carlow-Kilkenny Fianna Fáil have the only Carlow deputy and with the prospect of a full term before the next election there is obviously a great chance to muster a full Carlow quota. This should make two Kilkenny seats possible even with a divided approach. Wexford is obviously a marginal constituency which could go either way depending on conditions at the time of an election.

In spite, then, of all the prognostications, the magnitude of the Fianna Fáil defeat has not been unprecedented. From the point of view of actual electoral support so recently established by the only credible opinion poll, the party is favourably positioned for a come-back, all things being equal. Not alone is it the largest party with only a few extra seats necessary for an overall majority, but this election itself provides evidence that this result is readily obtainable. It is clear that, bad as circumstances were, defeat could have been averted if there had been unity of purpose, smooth organisation, a modicum of the old morale and a genuine effort in the constituencies to achieve maximum representation regardless of personalities. In the event the only retarding factors in the Fianna Fáil decline were the fierce self-preservation instinct of the candidates and the continuing resistance of the people to a Fine Gael government, however low Fianna Fáil may have sunk. This time the party was rent asunder going into the election; the state of the economy was disastrous and Fianna Fáil was clearly very largely to blame for this; and without exception the professional political experts insisted their leader had the lowest rating in public esteem of any political party leader since 1922. Yet their electoral support fell lower in 1954 with a completely united party sustained by a high level of morale, with the state of the economy half way to being restored after the first Coalition government and with the most illustrious political leader in the history of the State. Not alone that but the experts have decided, again unanimously, that the Fine Gael leader is the unique possessor of both a charisma and a halo, and they ought to know because they constructed and presented both of these mystical things themselves. If all this is true, the only logical verdict on the election outcome is that it was a signal failure for Fine Gael and, as a matter of fact, that is also what the figures say — horns and cloven feet have triumphed over a charisma and halo. Can they ever expect to have more favourable circumstances unless Fianna Fáil actually disintegrates as, admittedly, it seems likely to do, having done everything else to help? There are many people thoroughly disgusted with Fianna Fáil who, when it comes to the point on election day cannot bring themselves to vote for Fine Gael, charismas, haloes, cloven feet and horns notwithstanding. Apart from their record on the national issue dating from the acceptance of the boundary agreement, even young people remember the heavy gang and their fathers and grandfathers remember the earlier brutality associated with Oriel House. These older people also remember the Blueshirts. They will certainly get further reminders of Fine Gael characteristics this time and this will be one factor helping Fianna Fáil at the next election. The outcome for the economy of the fact that the policy is not going to be that put forward by Fine Gael nor a socialist policy, is likely to be another such factor.

This will hardly be enough, however, if there is not a cleansing of the party. There are some prominent members of the parliamentary party who should be in Fine Gael and there are others who are unsuitable to be public representatives at all. As well as that there is the question of a real will to win in every constituency and this is the essential ingredient of a realistic attempt to attain a majority. Fianna Fáil have only one seat out of three in six constituencies. They have one out of four in two constituencies, one out of five in two constituencies and two out of five in ten constituencies. They have a majority in ten constituencies — two out of three in seven and three out of five in three. In the other eleven they have two out of four. When, as in Fianna Fáil at present, there is an absence of idealism, the greatest difficulty facing a party trying to achieve a majority is to get a genuine effort for an extra seat in constituencies where they are in a minority. The preservation of one's own seat becomes the most important consideration in these circumstances. In fact, I have known cases of deputies who preferred to be in opposition as they could be against everything unpopular and in favour of every demand by any section of the public. Once a party gets into a minority position in a constituency there is a vested interest against breaking out of that situation, irrespective of the efforts of party headquarters. Considering the case where there is only one Fianna Fáil deputy out of three, the sitting depty will know that, if he acquires a colleague at the next election, there is always the danger that one or other of them will lose out at a subsequent election. This means, in effect, that the greatest danger to his seat is the achieving of a majority in his constituency. The day of victory may well be and often has proved to be the beginning of defeat and political oblivion for the original incumbent, particularly if the victory came in a by-election. Human nature, therefore, would tend to make his effort to acquire a new colleague less than whole-hearted and the current crop of Fianna Fáil TDs are very 'human' indeed. If, as seems likely, there is to be a four year period of Coalition government, the single deputy has four years to gain control of his constituency organisation so as to be in a position to nobble the convention for the next election for the purpose of ensuring his running-mates will be no danger to himself — or to the opposition. There have been cases of this in the past, known to everyone concerned with organisation on the national scale, where the organisation became a purely personal instrument centred on the existing deputy, with the result that there was great difficulty in getting a viable second or third candidate selected. This tendency is always there for every party but now that Fianna Fáil has become what it is, with personal organisations in every constituency, it will be even more difficult to get a genuine effort to break out of a minority position in individual constituencies and, therefore, it will be correspondingly difficult to get a real effort for a majority on a national scale. This factor operates also where the position is two seats out of five but, with two people involved, it may be more difficult to control and manipulate the organisation. The ridiculous interpretation by the constituency commission of the riduculous guideline laid down by the Fianna Fáil government that five seat constituencies should be related to areas of dense population, facilitates the rigging of such constituencies to safeguard a two-out-of-five situation thereby creating a stagnant minority. A perfect example is Limerick East where it has apparently become an unwritten law of the Fianna Fáil organisation that there is to be one city deputy and one rural deputy leaving no scope for the dual-purpose candidate (particularly if he supports the leader). If they happened to win a seat in a by-election, the fat would be in the fire. In a one-out-of-four or one-out-of-five situation the danger posed to the incumbent by the winning of a second seat is not so great and improvement is, therefore, more feasible. In present circumstances there will be the additional factor of holding the fort either for the loyalists or the dissidents. The situation in Fianna Fáil being as it is, the calibre of the deputies so low and their motivation so shallow, magnifies the task of making a come-back even if the leadership question is settled.

The salient feature of the defeat of Fianna Fáil in November 1982, the feature which appears to herald a further decline, is that it was engineered from within. The sequence of events started with a deliberately public move against the Taoiseach, who was only half a year in office, at a very critical time for the country (both parts) and at a time when the party's position as a goverment was balanced on a knife-edge. It was based on the continuing personal campaign against the Taoiseach's character. It was, of course, a decision to bring down the government. It would be ludicrous to expect to topple the Taoiseach and to be allowed, by the necessary outside support, to continue with a Fianna Fáil government under leadership not put before the people. The independent deputies involved would have to be insane to fall for that. In the event, the conspirators presented an even worse spectacle than the image of the Taoiseach, which had so painstakingly been established. How many factions are there? Two? Three? or Four? There was no question in anyone's mind of there being only one. If the putsch was successful how many more potential successors were there waiting in the wings for the inevitable realisation that any of the front-runners would wreck the party? The media men assembled, for public edification, an assortment of unprepossessing compromise candidates — each showing either the general characteristic of deviousness or no characteristic at all. One thing appeared clear — there were at most two in the cabinet that Mr Haughey could really trust, possibly only one and maybe in a real crunch none. As events stood, with the boat already heaving in heavy seas, the consideration of not rocking the boat would probably have achieved much the same result as the open vote. Adherence to the leader, however, was based purely on pragmatism. One wonders was there one fully committed supporter in the parliamentary party.

It seemed to me that the most interesting thing about this whole chain of events culminating in the election was the sudden change it produced in the Taoiseach. His performance from the moment the party Motion of No-Confidence was publicly announced (although intended to be decided secretly), but particularly in the actual campaign must have gone a long way to counter the effect of the chronic indecisiveness, the deviousness and the weakness he had demonstrated since May 1970. It did not do enough to establish full credibility on the national issue. This wasn't possible; the physical evidence of a hundred per cent participation in the British military effort was there for all to see and this could not be overcome. It is Fianna Fáil's achievement that politicians taking their stance on a watered-down version of the unanimously adopted Costello–deValera Motion — the only policy statement on the Six County question formally adopted by the Dáil — are now cynically dismissed as 'playing the Green Card'. How could any of the existing professional politicians, with the single exception of Neil Blaney, expect to be taken seriously in this respect in view of the evidence on the ground? My opinion was that Mr Haughey's reaction to his defeat on the confidence motion in the Dáil should have been to do no more than the consititution required, namely, to place his resignation in the hands of the President, to make no request for a dissolution and leave it to his opponents inside and outside the party to place their confidence in the Fine Gael leader and sit back to watch developments. I still think that would have been wiser but apparently his blood was up. He had been rejuvenated by the McCreevy sabotage attempt, had dug his heels in and decided at long last to face his enemies and fight, and contrary to all the evidence of the past twelve years, he still had a fight in him. It was a most impressive performance.

All the circumstances were against him. The reputation he had so deliberately, so carefully, methodically and professionally built up was in shreds. The economy was in dire straits. His deals were seen to be irresponsible and reckless. The internal opposition to him had been quantified and exposed in a fair amount of detail to the public and he knew that the personal campaign against him from that source would be more virulent this time. His reaction was to decide to expose himself completely by publishing not only a severe hairshirt programme for some years ahead but also the estimates for the coming year and to fight from that stark position. It turned out to be virtually a single-handed fight. His supporters had not the capacity for the task and anyone who had the ability to give him some effective support withheld it. Bearing in mind his hemmed-in defensive position and the comprehensive disposition of the attack, his television and press conference performances were masterly. He reminded me of a boxer reeling on the ropes but suddenly fighting his way back to the centre of the ring, still trading punches at the final bell and losing on a split decision instead of the expected knock-out.

In the latter stages of the campaign he was handed what should have been a winning opportunity by the Prior-Fitzgerald introduction of the Six County issue into the campaign. He made the effort to avail of it and succeeded to the extent of seeing his opponent whinging that a normal and patently reasonable challenge on a political matter introduced by himself, at a time when the election campaign was peaking, was an attack on his personal character (and he with a halo donated by the media on his head). Because of the twelve year record, however, this had only a marginal effect which produced one seat at most. The only constituencies where there was a pro-Fianna Fáil swing were those comprising the three Ulster counties, where the people know what the RUC and UDR are and know also that there is no other source of supply of personnel for Dr Fitzgerald's proposed Corps of Third Policemen. Even in Ulster it was not possible to get a significant percentage of the 'H-Block vote'. It will take more than election talk to do that. In the other border constituencies of Louth and Sligo-Leitrim it was a case of getting three seats out of four and in the circumstances this was not possible. These are not, of course, border constituencies in the same sense as Donegal, Cavan and Monaghan. Louth and Leitrim have only comparatively short borders with the Six Counties. Donegal is almost cut off from the rest of the Twenty-six County State by the border, while all parts of Cavan and Monaghan would be readily accessible to the Third Policemen. If Fine Gael have their way, these areas will constitute the major part of the buffer zone.

What a pity both for the party and the economy, if not for the integrity of the country, that Mr Haughey's regeneration as a fighting man did not come when he was first elected as party leader and Taoiseach! He could with credibility and with a reasonable prospect of success have tackled the disaster of the 1977 Manifesto at that time. He could also, even at that very late stage, have restored some credibility to Fianna Fáil as the Republican party, restored respectability to the concept of Republicanism and, at the same time, clearly identified to the world the only way in which the violence in the Six Counties could be ended. To attempt to get back the lost aura at the tail end of a desperate election campaign was too much to expect. He could have nipped in the bud the disruptive movement that seems likely to bring the split in Fianna Fáil, which should have come for more worthy reasons twelve years ago. Instead he allowed the Manifesto nonsense to proceed; conceded every demand made by Mrs Thatcher without seeking the slightest concession in Britain's 'not an inch' policy; and meekly accepted even the public renunciation of his leadership by Mr Colley days after he was appointed Tanaiste.

At the end of 1982 the intrinsic quality of the Fianna Fáil party has not been improved. Mr Haughey, himself, is a changed man. It remains to be seen if the change will persist and whether the breathing space in opposition will be used to attempt to cleanse the party and maybe even to reconstitute it as the national movement. This is a major undertaking.

It seems that it must involve the loss of some personnel who belong to Fianna Fáil the Pragmatic Party, but not to Fianna Fáil the Republican Party, but it also involves the restoration of the qualities the party has lost over the years. This is a two-part operation. First of all the idealism, integrity, sense of national purpose and, therefore, of self-confidence must become a reality throughout all levels of the organisation and then, or preferably concurrently, a deeply cynical electorate must be convinced that this metamorphosis has taken place. This is the essential change if they are to regain their standing in the public estimation but it seems to me it is also something that is beyond the capacity of the party as it stands. If the regeneration of Mr Haughey proves not to be of a transient nature, it can be taken for granted that matters of policy will be promoted with the greatest possible competence and that no amount of media antagonism will disguise his superior stature compared with his opponents. What I am saying, in other words, is that there is no doubt of his capacity for dealing competently with every political argument. The trouble is that, because of his own actual performance over the past twelve years, the fundamental task of restoring the moral fibre of the party will not be within his personal capacity. Someone else is needed for that part of the job and there is no one else. If he handles the problem of disaffection in the party firmly and successfully, he can clearly maintain the pattern since 1973 of alternating Coalition and Fianna Fáil governments. Unfortuantely this is not good enough either for the rehabilitation of Fianna Fáil or for the good of the country, and I mean the country not the Twenty-six County State.

Appendix A

The following resolution for the 1971 Ard Fheis was submitted by a number of units of the organisation:

> This Ard Fheis RE-DEDICATES the Fianna Fáil party
> to the first aim as stated in the Coru and, while recognis-
> ing that, in order to achieve this, it is essential to bring
> about a real unification of the sections of the Irish
> people at present divided and that this cannot be done
> and should not be attempted by the use of force:—
>
> (a) REJECTS the suggestion that a local majority
> in any part of Ireland has the right to opt out of
> the Irish nation or that any outside parliament
> has the right to exercise jurisdiction over any
> part of the national territory as defined in
> Bunreacht na hÉireann.
>
> (b) REAFFIRMS the responsibility of the British
> parliament for the injustice inflicted on this
> country by Partition and for all the evils of dis-
> crimination, victimisation, violence and
> bloodshed that have arisen and continue to
> arise from that injustice.
>
> (c) REJECTS the claim of the British government
> that the Six Counties are part of the United
> Kingdom, and
>
> (d) CALLS ON the British government to
> announce its intention of embarking on the
> process of disengaging from this country.

The fate of this resolution is described in *We Won't
Stand (Idly) By* as follows:

> It was, not surprisingly, superseded as Resolution 1 by
> the following: 'The Ard Fheis records its confidence in
> the Taoiseach and the government and assures them of
> unwavering support in their efforts to end Partition by
> peaceful means in accordance with the traditional policy
> of Fianna Fáil.'
> This undoubtedly had the merit of greater simplicity

and it was undoubtedly more attuned to the mood of the majority of the delegates who did not want details, who did not want discussion, who wanted merely to endorse the 'leader' and go home.

The only aspect of the traditional Fianna Fáil policy deemed worthy of mention was 'peaceful means'. This was an aspect which no one within the party opposed to the best of my knowledge. But the omission of important parts of the Resolution which did attempt to actually outline 'traditional Fianna Fáil policy' and the failure to detail the current, authentic policy in regard to these aspects was highly significant.

In the bogus resolution appearing on the Clár, all of the preamble after the word Coru as well as sections (b) and (c) were censored. The same tactics by the chair were repeated. No view opposing that of the leadership was allowed and our effort to deal with our resolution in detail, point by point, by a succession of three-minute speeches, was submerged in the new type of democracy established at this Ard Fheis. Resolution No. 1 was carried.

As far as I was concerned the matter was now decided. Rigged or not this was the Fianna Fáil Ard Fheis. It was the appropriate body to change the policy of the party. It was the only body which had the authority to decide fundamental policy and it had done so. It had done it without being allowed to hear the case argued but the issues were well known in advance and the Ard Fheis did not decide in ignorance of exactly what was involved. The decision was, in effect, that Fianna Fáil policy was whatever the leadership at any time said it was.

Taken in conjunction with Resolution No. 1 the previous year there was an unequivocal acceptance and endorsement of all the disputed statements and actions of the past two years. In addition, the pledge of continuing support for the future in these circumstances was an acceptance of the cult of the 'Infallible Leader'.

Fianna Fáil had, by the decision of its assembled delegates from every part of the Twenty-six Counties in which it operates and is the government party, altered its character from Republican to Free State. It now accepted the *bona fides* of the British government which continued to claim part of the national territory as defined in the Constitution as an integral part of the United Kingdom and which continued to guarantee the permanence of Partition. It now accepted that there was no real invader in Ireland at a time when the British army was engaged in blatant repression of what used to be recognised as the 'part of the national majority coerced into the United Kingdom' but what was now in the new terminology called 'the minority in Northern Ireland'. It now accepted that Partition was an Irish problem to be solved 'among us'. It now rejected the view that Partition was 'perhaps the gravest injury one nation could inflict on another'. It now rejected the view that the essential requirement to remedy the injustice was a British decision to undo this wrong.

There was, in fact, now no wrong. In short it rejected everything it had originally held as fundamental principles and accepted the policy of the old Cumann na nGaedheal Free State Party.

Fianna Fáil has truly become the 'Party of Reality' and the reality is that there are two States in this island and it is in this context that Fianna Fáil subsists as the government party of one of the two States, with all the perquisites and status that go with it.

Appendix B

This is dealt with in *We Won't Stand (Idly) By* as follows:

Representatives of the Stormont administration made a very poor showing and everyone was feeling happy that the case was going well until Mr Martin J. Hillenbrand, Assistant Secretary of State for European Affairs, appeared to put the case against the Resolution. Suddenly Congressman Frelinghuysen's question about the attitude of the Irish government was answered. Mr Hillenbrand was able to show by quotations from the Taoiseach's speech at the 1972 Fianna Fáil Ard Fheis that the Irish government was opposed to the terms of the Resolution.

He concluded his submission as follows: 'In the present circumstances of Ireland I think that the Prime Minister's (Mr Lynch) statement is impressive and courageous. It expresses an attitude which I believe Americans who have Ireland's best interests at heart could adopt as a model. In the spirit of that attitude I think we should refrain from making declarations which to echo the Prime Minister's words, could generate exaggerated expectations which are beyond our power to fulfil and which, therefore, would not advance the interests of Ireland, but could, in fact, set them back.'

During his submission he made the following statement: 'Therefore, U.N. good offices, like U.S. good offices, could only be useful in a situation in which both parties agree that they ought to be requested. This precondition applies *a fortiori* to proposals for U.N. fact-finding missions or peace-keeping forces, and we note that the Irish government has not pressed for such U.N. actions.'

Congressman Murphy, who throughout the hearing was most assiduous in asking questions in support of the Resolution, was quick to ask Mr Hillenbrand if he had heard him correctly as saying that the Irish government had not pressed for U.N. action as he was only one of a number of Congressmen and Senators in the room who were present when the Irish Foreign Minister had told a joint meeting of members of both Houses that he had pressed Mr Rodgers in this regard. Mr Hillenbrand repeated that this did not happen.

The attitude of the Irish government had now been disclosed to the Committee. The Irish people present had to endure the humiliation of hearing the case in refutation of the Resolution based on the Taoiseach's address to the Ard Fheis and on Dr Hillery's visit to the Secretary of State. The Taoiseach's interview with the *Washington Post* confirmed this attitude.

It appeared to me to be significant that it was while Mr Hillenbrand was testifying that the Irish ambassador appeared for the first time. We knew, of course, what the attitude was but it was still a shock to hear this Resolution which so adequately expressed the Irish case being demolished by reference to the attitude of the Irish government. Irish Republicans had for so long been trying to get American opinion and influence behind our case for freedom and unity.

Suddenly, without any effort on our part, but arising from the struggle of the Six County nationalist population against British repression, one of the most powerful voices in America — that of Senator Ted Kennedy, widely believed to be a future President — was raised on our behalf. The Irish government had shown its annoyance by ignoring it. The British reaction showed how sensitive they were to American criticism and pressure but there was no follow up from the Irish government and now the case against the Resolution was based on the Irish government's attitude.

Appendix C

The report of the Committee on the Constitution, December 1967, is dealt with as follows in *We Won't Stand (Idly) By:*

> The Christian preamble, the special position of the Catholic Church, the prohibition on divorce, the re-introduction of the Senate among other things were designed to secure if not the active support at least the neutrality or non-belligerence of various groups of people so that the fundamental purpose of stating the Republican claim in the basic law of the State would not be frustrated. The first three Articles in particular are a formal and perfect statement of the national claim and they are re-inforced and amplified by the next eight.
>
> Article One makes an affirmation of sovereignty on behalf of 'the Irish Nation'.
>
> Article Two defines the national territory as the 'whole island of Ireland, its islands and the territorial seas'.
>
> No change is proposed in either of these two Articles but Article Three is recommended for deletion and re-placement, the only reason given for the deletion of what is in it being that the members of the Committee feel it would now be appropriate.
>
> It says much for the tenacity of Fine Gael that, after thirty years, they still deemed it 'appropriate' to return to the pre-1937 position, in which the Boundary Agreement had the sanction of the Twenty-six County parliament. For Fianna Fáil to deem it 'appropriate' that the vaunted Republican achievement of 1937 should be un-done and that we should revert to the Free State position is surely evidence of the renunciation of Republicanism in the pre-Lynch sense.
>
> Article 3 of the Constitution reads as follows: 'Pending the re-integration of the national territory, and without prejudice to the right of the Parliament and Government established by this Constitution to exercise juris-

diction over the whole of that territory, the laws enacted by that Parliament shall have the like area and extent of application as the laws of Saorstat Éireann and the like extra-territorial effect.'

The problem in drafting the Article was to explain away the factual area of jurisdiction without betraying Republican principles. As enacted, the Article represents the maximum concession to the *status quo* established by the Government of Ireland Act, the Treaty and the Civil War, which it was possible to reconcile with the Republican principle. It makes no concession to the Boundary Agreement ratified by the Free State Dáil before the formation of Fianna Fáil. The vital thing in the Article is the assertion that the limited area of application of the laws is without prejudice to the right to exercise jurisdiction over the whole of the national territory as defined in the previous Article. The historic claim of the Irish people is thus made at the outset of the Constitution and the action of the people's delegates in 1925 is annulled.

The Committee's proposal is to restore the position as it existed before 1937. The suggestion, if carried out, would, of course, do more because the specific withdrawal of the claim made in 1937, twelve years after the Boundary Agreement, would make the endorsement of Partition all the more definite — and the only reason given for this astounding reactionary proposal by representatives of the three established political parties in the Twenty-six Counties is that they 'deem it appropriate'!

One might ask is not the real reason that they have all acquired a vested interest in the partitioned State in which they operate — in the separate set of institutions. The suggested replacement of Article 3 is as follows:—

'1. The Irish Nation hereby affirms its firm will that its territory be re-united in harmony and brotherly affection between all Irishmen.

'2. The laws enacted by the Parliament established by this Constitution shall, until the achievement of the nation's unity shall otherwise require, have the

like area and extent of application as the laws of the
Parliament which existed prior to the adoption of this
Constitution. Provison may be made by law to give
extra-territorial effect to such laws.'

The reason for the final sentence is explained but
there is silence about the rest. Note the tactful avoid-
ance of any mention of 'Saorstat Éireann', entailing the
use of eleven words instead of two, although the purpose is to re-establish the Saorstat without the use of the
emotive title so redolent of 'battles long ago'.

No one could object to the sentiment of harmony and
brotherly affection. The sell-out consists of the
suggested deletion of the assertion that the limited area
of application of the laws is without prejudice to the
right to exercise jurisdiction over the whole of the
national territory and the substitution of the statement
that this shall be the area of jurisdiction 'until the
achievement of the nation's unity shall otherwise require'.

The recommendation is that the claim in justice to
national unity should be dropped, as it was dropped in
1925, and replaced by the 'aspiration to unity', which
has since been promulgated as Republican Party and
national policy by the Taoiseach.

The dropping of this claim is the abandonment of
Republicanism. If adopted, the recommendation of Mr
Colley's Committee would completely sabotage the case
of the Six-County Republicans. It is a reversal of the
principles on which Fianna Fáil was founded; it is recommended by two present Fianna Fáil ministers and by
two parliamentary secretaries and although it was published almost five years ago the 'Republican Party' has
not rejected it at any level.

This document was circulated some time in the latter
half of December 1967. The papers were immediately
full of its comments and recommendations about
divorce and the special position of the Catholic Church
but there was no mention of Article 3. That was just
'something about the national territory', which could
not be of any importance and when the Committee

themselves did not think it worthy of comment why should the 'media' bother. Of course, this is the way to slip a thing through — put it in the small print without explanation and hope no one notices it.

I did not get an opportunity to look at the Report until Christmas Eve. I read as far as the end of page seven when it began to deal with inconsequential matters such as the institution of President. I had read thus far with feelings of disbelief and outrage. When it started to waffle about the President I decided I had seen enough and that it was absolutely essential that as honorary secretary of the party, as a deputy and as a minister, I must publicly disassociate myself from all the recommendations as far as I had read at the first opportunity — and in particular the recommendation in regard to Article 3.

I had often been glad of the 'loyalty' of the members of Fianna Fáil when I had to explain unpopular decisions, but I assumed there were some who read and who examined things critically. I consequently expected at the very least queries about this recommendation but apparently people were prepared to accept the media comments as covering what was in the Report, and discussion was about such things as divorce only.

I telephoned the secretary of Ballyfermot Comhairle Ceanntair on Christmas Day, told him I wanted a meeting called so that I could disown this document, and we agreed that the earliest possible date would be 2 January 1968. I prepared my script, making my position clear.

Unfortunately, there was a government meeting before the meeting at which I was to speak and I decided I should raise the matter there first. Accordingly, I gave the Taoiseach a copy of what I proposed to say and suggested that it would be better that the government as a whole should reject the recommendation. The Taoiseach was appalled at the prospect of one minister publicly rejecting what had been recommended by another minister, but I insisted that I must disown this immediately. Eventually, I agreed to his request to see if I could tone down the speech while still satisfying myself that I had publicly dissented.

This was not easy but I spent some hours on it and eventually the script I circulated was as follows: 'The informal Committee on the Constitution, which has recently published its Report, was composed of twelve individual deputies and senators who are members of the three political parties represented in Dáil Éireann. It should be understood that they were not appointed as delegates or plenipotentiaries from their parties nor had they any discussions with their parties on the various matters which they discussed and reported on.

'The other members of the parties were not, in fact, aware what particular provisions of the Constitution were under discussion. The Committee, themselves, made it clear in their Report that the views expressed and the recommendations made were their own opinions only and could not be taken as representing the views of their political parties. Nevertheless, there is an understandable tendency on the part of the public to regard the recommendations which they made unanimously as accurately expressing the views of the Oireachtas members at least.

'As it is likely to be some time before the government or the Fianna Fáil party consider their attitude to the various matters in this Report, I want to make it clear that there is no commitment whatever on our part to the views expressed by this Committee — even where they were, apparently, unanimous. All that can be said is that four Fianna Fáil deputies and two senators hold these views. Nothing is known about the views of the remainder.

'The Constitution as enacted by the people in 1937 was not a hastily conceived document. It was produced over five years of Fianna Fáil government and the need at the time was to replace a Constitution imposed with the 1922 Treaty and containing many provisions which could not be reconciled with the national aspirations of the Irish people. A lot of thought went into the compilation of the draft constitution which was eventually submitted to the people and accepted by them as covering as satisfactorily as possible the situation, which had been established without compromising the national position.

'Public comment so far has been only in reference to those parts of the Committee's Report which became known in advance of publication. It is important that the fact that there has not been any comment by members of the government or the Fianna Fáil party either on these matters or the other recommendations made should not be taken as indicating agreement with all or any of these recommendations. Our members' minds will be set at rest if they bear in mind the Aims of the party as laid down in the Coru and the many resolutions unanimously passed at successive Ard Fheiseanna.'